Assemblies for Infants

BOOK 1

Diane Walker

RMEP

RELIGIOUS AND MORAL EDUCATION PRESS

To Margaret and Trevor,
with love and gratitude.
And, as ever, to Robin,
Rebekah and Rachael,
with my love.

Published by Religious and Moral Education Press
A division of SCM-Canterbury Press Ltd
A wholly owned subsidiary of Hymns Ancient & Modern Ltd
St Mary's Works, St Mary's Plain
Norwich, Norfolk NR3 3BH

First published 1999

ISBN 1 85175 170 X

Designed and typeset by Topics – The Creative Partnership, Exeter

Illustrations by Brian Platt

Printed in Great Britain by Brightsea Ltd, Exeter

Contents

Contents (continued)

Introduction

Assemblies/Collective worship

The term 'assembly' is used throughout this book for ease of reference. An 'assembly' is not necessarily the same as an 'act of worship', often applying to the 'school business' requirements of the meeting, rather than to its religious content. However, 'assembly' remains the more widely used term.

Pupil integrity

Perhaps the most important factor to be taken into consideration when planning and delivering an assembly is that of pupil integrity. The position of each pupil must be respected, and agreement with views expressed or with religious statements made in the assembly should never be assumed. Statements of belief should always be introduced with distancing phrases, such as 'Christians believe ...' and 'This is an important belief to Christians ...'. This will respect and preserve the integrity of both teacher (presenter) and pupil. This practice is to be observed particularly at prayer-time. Pupils should not be compelled to join in with prayers, or to chorus the 'Amen' automatically, but should be given a choice. The prayer should be introduced with a phrase such as 'I am now going to say a Christian prayer. You may join in with the "Amen" at the end if you wish.' The prayers in this book are not preceded by such a phrase each time, and some invite pupil participation. But the fact that this is an invitation, and not an order, should be made abundantly clear to the pupils each time. At the same time, it should be made clear also that all of the pupils are expected to listen quietly and with respect: it is a two-way consideration. For the same reasons, the home situation of the pupils should always be borne in mind. Their participation in any part of the assembly which would compromise or oppose the ethos and beliefs expressed at home should be avoided. Similarly, any response from the pupils to the material which is itself respectful of different interpretations and is itself appropriately expressed should be accepted and valued.

Prayers and reflections

Each assembly includes either a prayer or a reflection, or both. As stated above, the prayer should be introduced with a distancing phrase such as 'Listen quietly while I read a Christian prayer. If you wish to, you can join in the "Amen" at the end.' Some of the prayers involve the pupils' participation, whether directly or indirectly. This should not be assumed or demanded.

Reflections are intended to fulfil a different purpose. They invite the pupils to think privately about an issue. Pupils should not be expected to share these thoughts, although some may choose to do so later. It should be made clear to them that this is a private time.

Often, a focal point is suggested, for both the prayers and the reflections. These suggestions are intended to encourage more focused attention from the pupils. Where no focal point is suggested, more general ones can be incorporated by the presenter, such as a lighted candle, a display, a view of the sky through a window. It is helpful to institute a recognized signal to mark the end of any thinking time. This could be a chord on the piano, a soft handclap or an agreed phrase, spoken quietly.

Preparation and planning

Many of these assemblies require only the minimum of preparation. Some do require more, but this is eased by the 'You will need' section at the beginning of the assembly. Every leader is called upon at some time to present an assembly with little or no warning. It is hoped that there are ample assemblies in this collection which would lend themselves to this 'one-off' requirement. At the same time, it is preferable that, wherever possible, each assembly fits into a prearranged plan, and that records are kept of assemblies presented. To this end, the assemblies are arranged thematically. Within each section, some assemblies are linked or form a mini-sequence, so enabling development and reinforcement of the theme. Some assemblies, of course, relate to the themes of more than one section. To enable easier cross-referencing, a thematic index has been included, and some links with other sections are indicated at the end of assemblies.

Contents of the sections

Most sections consist of the following parts:
You will need: this lists the items required during the presentation of the assembly.
Introduction: this is usually the part of the assembly which grounds the material in and relates it to the pupils' own experience. This is essential if the material is to have any relevance or meaning to them.
Core material: from the base of the Introduction, the next part of the assembly seeks to encourage the pupils to explore the theme in a wider Christian context. The core material presents the assembly's theme and explores its implications.
Prayer/Reflection: see above.
There are some exceptions to this basic plan, for instance the music and the outdoor assemblies.

Pupil participation

Pupil participation is built into the vast majority of the assemblies. It takes varying forms and degrees, ranging from the simple answering of questions, through singing, cooking and miming, to preparing and sharing their own work. Again, the pupils' integrity must be respected when selection is made. In some assemblies, the prayers involve pupil participation also.

Variety of content

The content of the assemblies is varied, and seeks to introduce a variety of stimuli to capture the pupils' interest and encourage their own consideration of the theme. These stimuli include stories of other countries, poetry, nature and natural phenomena, other people, stories and history, everyday things, music and festivals.

Atmosphere

A conducive atmosphere immediately before, during and after an assembly is vital if the pupils are to approach the assembly in a suitable frame of mind. Many schools have to use the assembly time to convey important information or news to the pupils. When this is the case, it is helpful to have a clear dividing line between the business part of the gathering and the 'worship' part. A change of presenter helps, or a statement that one part is over and the other beginning. A display or object which the pupils come to associate with assemblies – such as a table reserved for this use which could hold a focal point such as flowers or a candle – could be helpful in differentiating this use of the room from its other uses. Appropriate music for the pupils to enter and leave by helps to set this time apart from the normal business of the day and the room.

Music suggestions

Suggested songs related to the theme of each section are listed on page 113. More general or familiar songs can, of course, be substituted.

Health and safety

Teachers are referred to their Health and Safety documents when any activity is suggested – especially during the outdoor assemblies, and when making objects.

Indexes

There are two indexes: one is a thematic index to simplify the search for an assembly on a particular theme, and the other is an index of the people and places mentioned in the assemblies. The contents page itself contains information about the content of each assembly.

Literacy

Much of the oral work and the activities in these assemblies complement the requirements of the Literacy Programme.

Acknowledgements

The material on pages 12–13 is adapted from *Our Daily Bread*, a booklet of teaching materials published by The Missions to Seamen, St Michael Paternoster Royal, College Hill, London EC4R 2RL, and is used with their kind permission.

The material on pages 28–31 is used with the kind permission of The Toybox Charity, P.O. Box 660, Amersham, Bucks HP6 6EA.

The material on page 33 is used with the kind permission of World Vision U.K., 599 Avebury Boulevard, Milton Keynes MK9 3PG.

The material on pages 37 and 39 is based on stories from Christian Aid, used with their kind permission.

The information and logo on pages 40–41 and 116 are used with the kind permission of Samaritan's Purse International/Operation Christmas Child, Victoria House, Victoria Road, Buckhurst Hill, Essex IG9 5EX.

The material on pages 50–51 is used with the kind permission of Hearing Dogs for Deaf People.

The songs 'How?' (page 102) and 'God Goes with Us' (page 109) are used with the kind permission of Nick Harding/The Time Travelling! Project.

The song 'Harambee' (page 103) is copyright © McCrimmon Publishing Co. Ltd, used with their kind permission.

The song 'Jesus the Lord Said' (pages 107 and 108) is used with the kind permission of Marshall Pickering (HarperCollins Publishers).

1 Sukkot: The Feast of Tabernacles

Introduction

Ask how many of the pupils have spent a holiday in a tent or played in tents in the garden. Talk about living in a tent, and about the differences between this and their 'normal' life in their houses. Do they think life is easier in a tent or harder? Do any adults present agree or disagree with the pupils? Invite some pupils to mime jobs people have to do when they are staying in a tent, such as putting up the tent, hammering in tent-pegs, blowing up airbeds, carrying water, cooking on a small cooker on the ground, washing clothes and pots. It isn't easy! But many people still like to stay in tents for their holidays: ask the pupils if they can suggest why this is so. Living in a tent can be like an adventure, especially for children. Ask if there are any things the pupils particularly like, or think they would like, about staying in a tent.

Do any of them know what tents are made of? Talk about the materials and qualities required, especially waterproofness. The Jewish people have used 'tents' made of something else for many hundreds of years – and some of them still do! But they only use these tents for a certain part of the year. Jewish families have a lot of fun while they are staying in these tents: but they do it for a serious and important reason. It is to remind them of what God has done for them. The tents they stay in are made of tree branches! These special tents are called 'booths'.

Many years before Jesus was born, the Jews did not have their own land. Instead, they were working as slaves in Egypt. God knew how unhappy they were, and he chose a man called Moses to lead them to a new land, where they could live in safety and freedom. But this new land was many miles from Egypt and the Jewish people had a long and dangerous journey to make with all their belongings and their animals. They had to live in tents, putting them up every time they reached a new place, and taking them down when they had used up all the grass and food there. They got hot and thirsty walking through the desert. Soon they ran out of water! The only water they could find was horrible – far too sour to drink. But God told Moses to throw a piece of wood into the water and when they tried the water again, it tasted just right. The next time they ran out of water, God told Moses to hit a big rock with his stick, and fresh water flowed out of the rock!

One day, they ran out of food too. God sent some birds to settle near the camp, and they were able to catch them. He also sent something that tasted like honey wafers and looked like bread. They travelled through the desert and the hills for forty years. But God always sent them food.

When they reached their new land, God told them to remember how he had saved them from Egypt, and how he had looked after them on their journey. He said, 'At the end of the harvest, when you have all the fruit and the grain safely stored, make booths for yourselves, like tents, using the branches of trees. Leave your new homes for a whole week, and live in these booths instead. While you are doing this, remember what your life was like when you were living in tents all the time. Remember how I sent you food and water. Remember to tell others why you are doing this, and to thank me for looking after you then and for sending you food every year in your new country.'

Jews have done this every year since then. They still thank God for looking after them on their journey, and for giving them food every year.

PRAYER

Thank you, God, that you looked after your people all those years ago. Help us to say thank you for our food. Thank you that we can enjoy being in tents when we are playing or on holiday.

2 Harvest 1

You will need

- large-scale map of the world
- coloured 'post-it' notes, some cut into thin strips each with a strip of adhesive on it
- pieces of paper and felt-tips
- either: the Harvest display of food (check it includes different countries of origin)
  or: a small display of food chosen by you to show a variety of countries of origin

Note

Be aware of any food allergy in asking the pupils to handle unwrapped food.

Introduction

Comment as appropriate on the display of food. Ask the pupils if they know where any of it came from. Some will probably answer that it came from their homes or from shops: explain that you want to know where it came from before that – where it grew.

Choose two pupils to work at the map, showing them how the 'post-it' notes can mark countries without harming the map. Perhaps another adult could help these pupils, to liberate the presenter of the assembly. Tell the pupils that these two children are going to mark the countries that the food came from. Choose an example such as a tin of fruit. Read out its country of origin, point to it on the map so that it can be marked, then show how far from our country it is. Ask individual pupils to come and choose different foods until you have a good selection of countries represented. Set these foods to one side as the pupils work through them. Read out the names of the countries of origin as you show them where they are. Comment on the variety of countries and on their relative distances from us.

Harvest 1

If necessary, return foods grown in this country to the display. Recap on which foods have come from elsewhere. Ask if any of the pupils like these foods – are any of their favourites among them? If not, ask what some of their favourite foods are. If these are in the display, add them to the pile of foods from other countries and mark their countries of origin on the map. If not, simply write their names or draw them on a piece of paper, add it to the pile and mark the country of origin, if known, on the map.

Ask the pupils if they would like never to eat any of these foods (from abroad) again. Ask them to think about life without tasting baked beans, chocolate, etc., ever again. If there are adults present, ask them if they would like never to taste tea or coffee again.

Remind the pupils that most of this food came from our shops. Ask if any of them can remember going to a shop and finding that there was little or no food there. Our shops have plenty of food in them, and they have many different kinds of food in them. Once, people could only eat the foods which were 'in season': discuss what this means. Now, we can have a great variety of food all through the year. Even if we cannot get something like fresh strawberries, we can always get tinned or frozen ones. (If appropriate, you can talk about ways of preserving food here.)

> **Note**
>
> The map and markers will be needed for the next assembly – 'Harvest 2'

PRAYER

The pupils can write their own prayer for this assembly. Write the first line, as below, at the top of a sheet of paper and ask for favourite foods, for example:

Thank you, God, for the foods we love:
> Chocolate and baked beans,
> Apples and ...

3 Harvest 2

You will need

- the map and markers from the previous assembly – 'Harvest 1'

Introduction

Show the pupils the map, and remind them why some countries are marked on it. Remind them of some of the foods which came from these countries. Ask them how the food arrived in this country ready to be taken to the shops. Talk about possible ways of transporting food, and the need for some kinds of food – such as fresh fruit and fish – to travel more quickly than others – such as tinned meat and fruit. One of the main methods of transport is by ship. Ask pupils to think of all the food shops in their local town or city. Then ask them to think about all the shops in the whole country! There must be a lot of ships around to bring that much food to so many shops!

All the time – now and through the night – ships are travelling around the world moving food and other goods. This means that many sailors are travelling far from home, some of them on very long journeys. Some of them do not see their families for many months. They have to work hard on the ships, and when they finally arrive at a new country to unload their cargo of food or other goods, they do not know anybody there. Very often, they do not even speak the same language as the people who live there.

Being a sailor can be a very lonely life. But in many of the ports into which the ships sail, there are some people ready and waiting to greet the sailors – even though they do not know them! These people work for a society called The Missions to Seamen. They believe that God wants them to help sailors wherever they are. They have special buildings – like community centres and cafés – where the sailors can relax away from their ships, have a meal, and meet local people. They will hold church services here for the sailors to join in if they wish. Chaplains, people who work in the church, will go onto the ships to make sure that everyone is all right and to see if any of them need help. As well as all this, the Missions to Seamen will help if there is any sort of emergency. Here are some examples.

Thirty sailors from Cuba were stuck in Belfast when their ship broke down! It was nearly Christmas, and the sailors did not know anybody there. They had very little food and no money. The Missions to Seamen staff and people living in Belfast gave them food, money – and warm clothes.

If a sailor falls ill far from home, his ship might have to leave without him. He will be left in a strange country, with no one to visit him, and no one to talk to who knows his language. The Missions' staff will find someone who understands the sailor's language, and will make sure that he has visitors while he is in hospital.

One crew had been at sea for many months. The Missions' staff asked what they wanted most of all. Their answer? A haircut!

PRAYER

Listen as this prayer is read. The people who work at The Missions to Seamen's centres all over the world try to do this all the time.

In poverty and wealth
In sickness and in health
In good times and in bad
Whether happy or sad
We'll stand by you
And be your friend
In Jesus' name, for Jesus' sake.

(You may like to read this again after explaining any words you think need explaining.)

4 November 1

You will need

- a large sheet of paper, divided into four sections
- felt-tips
- a picture of snow in the country or town
- optional: pictures showing different seasons

Introduction

Talk about the different ways in which we divide up the year – into days, weeks, months and seasons. Talk about the relationship of these to each other.

Ask the pupils to name the four seasons. Write the names in order on the paper. Ask which months (roughly) fall into each season, and add these to the sections. Talk about the weather conditions associated with each season, or ask which pictures show which seasons. Ask the pupils to tell you what events they associate with each season and write these down in the appropriate places. Then ask them to think quietly about the four seasons in turn for a few minutes.

Ask which is their favourite season: ask for a show of hands for each. Decide with them which is the most popular. Then ask a few pupils to give reasons for their choice, covering each season which received a vote. Make a note, or draw a picture, of each reason in its appropriate season if not already included.

We have looked at the things we like about each season. Ask the pupils what they think people would say if they were asked what they do not like about each season. Add these suggestions to the chart in another colour. Some people might dislike things the pupils liked – such as snow! Discuss with them why other people might see the same thing so differently.

(It might be appropriate to develop the idea of snow and cold being problems for many people. The pupils might like to discuss ways in which their families could help people who feel threatened and isolated by poor weather conditions. Make sure that all suggestions are safe for pupils and that they are not encouraged to take action by themselves. Checking on elderly neighbours, and offering to shop for them are just two methods of help that a whole family could adopt.)

PRAYER

Show the pupils the picture of snow. Remind them that different people would have different feelings about it. Ask them to look at it while you read the prayer:

Father, we see beauty and excitement, play and adventure in snow.
Thank you for snow.
Others see coldness and danger, loneliness and fear.
Help us to remember this, and to see how we could help.

Note

The seasons chart will be needed for the next assembly – 'November 2'.

5 November 2

You will need

- a large sheet of paper, divided into four sections each headed with the name of a season
- the seasons chart completed in the last assembly – 'November 1'
- felt-tips

Introduction

In the last assembly, we looked at the things we liked about the seasons and the things people do not like about them. This poem (or extract) was written by someone who was thinking only of the things he did not like about a particular month – November. Ask the pupils which season this is in. Ask them what sort of weather we get in November. Talk about fogs. Read the lines:

> No sun – no moon!
> No morn – no noon –
> No dawn – no dusk – no proper time of day ...
> No shade, no shine, no butterflies, no bees,
> No fruits, no flowers, no leaves, no birds –
> November!

Extract from *November* by Thomas Hood

Ask the pupils to name some of the things the poet was complaining about. Once we start complaining about things, it is easy to find other things to complain about! Today we are going to write a poem together which will list the things we *do* like about the seasons.

(Depending on the age and ability of the pupils and the time available, a poem can be produced based on one or more of the seasons.)

Show the pupils the chart completed in the last assembly, and go through the things on it that they said they liked about each of the seasons (or just the one you have chosen). Ask if any of them have thought of anything else they can add. Explain that you will write the first line of each poem, and then add their lines. Remind them that poems do not have to rhyme. Begin with these lines, or your own, in the appropriate sections:

SPRING

Spring is

    yellow ducklings bobbing in the water

SUMMER

Summer is

    picnics on the beach

AUTUMN

Autumn is

    bonfires crackling

WINTER

Winter is

    snowball throwing in the garden

Build up four or five lines for each season, as appropriate. (Some pupils might like to produce pictures to add to the poems, or larger ones to display around it. Perhaps the poems could be displayed in a communal area or in each classroom in turn.)

PRAYER

Using the chart from the last assembly, remind the pupils of the things they said they liked about each season. Pupils can then be invited to make up simple prayers of thanks for these things. Give them an appropriate pattern to follow, such as

    Thank you, Father, for the daffodils in Spring.

6 Snowflakes

Note

Schools will not be able to use this assembly every year: *falling* snow is needed. Many schools will need to divide the pupils into smaller groups to derive full benefit, perhaps making this a class assembly. Pupils will need their outdoor clothes and shoes: perhaps this assembly could be done as soon as they arrive, while they are still wearing them. If they have very dark coats, they can use their sleeves for the activity: if not, each pupil will need a small piece of black card or paper.

You will need

- small pieces of black card – see above
- large sheet of paper – preferably black, with white or silver pens/pencils
- felt-tips, if paper is white

Core material

Outdoors

Tell the pupils to dress in their outdoor clothes. Impress on them any safety requirements dictated by the school's particular surroundings. Before they go out, explain that you are all going to catch snowflakes on sleeves or card and to look at them very closely. Just single flakes (or crystals) are needed: they might have to be patient until they catch several single flakes which they can see clearly. Remind them what will happen if they breathe on the flakes! Ask them to be thinking how they would describe the flakes: how many points do they have? (six) Can they find any the same? Do some have a more complicated pattern than others?

Take the pupils into the playground, showing them how to hold out sleeves or card. Allow them several minutes for this. You can discuss the flakes with them

Snowflakes

while they can still see them – depending on the temperature! Before they go in, ask them just to watch the flakes falling: how many do they think are falling just in their playground? Ask them to think about how many are falling all over your town, city or village. Do they think that anyone could count all of them?

Indoors

Once back inside, let the pupils take off their outdoor clothes and sit down. Ask them what they thought of the flakes. Were any the same? Were they able to count how many points each one had? Draw a sample flake on the paper: perhaps some of them would like to draw one too. Remind them how many points each flake should have. Some of them were so complicated that it would be very hard to draw an accurate picture of them.

Ask how many flakes they thought were falling in your area. Tell them that, if each of them had caught 100 flakes, they would all have been different. Snowflakes are never the same – even though millions and millions of them fall each time we have snow. Each one is different, and each one is special and unique. Discuss what unique means. Christians believe that each one of us is different from everyone else. Each one of us is special and unique. Even identical twins are not the same. Christians believe that God made us all different, just as he made the snowflakes different. They believe that he loves each one of us and sees beauty in every one of us – just as we can see beauty in each snowflake that falls.

PRAYER

Ask the pupils to think about how many children there are in the school, then in your town, in Britain, and all over the world. Remind them that Christians believe that God loves each child and that each child is special and unique.

Thank you, Father God, that I am special. Thank you that I am unique, and that you love me as a special person.

Note

This assembly could be followed up in the classroom by pupils making their own snowflakes for a display. These can be cut out of white paper to be displayed against a black background, or they can each paint a flake using white paint on black paper, having drawn an outline first for your approval. Younger pupils could be helped by having a framework of the points marked on their paper in pencil.

7 Memories 1

You will need

- a tray with a variety of objects on it, such as a pencil, a glove, an apple, a rubber, a book, etc.
- a piece of cloth to cover the tray
- a cotton handkerchief
- a 'post-it' note pad
- a collection of souvenirs, either genuine or 'made up', such as tickets, programmes, a pressed flower, a brochure or postcard, etc.
- a few seashells
- (if possible) pieces of lace – some handmade, a lacemaker's pillow or at least a lacemaker's bobbin – copies of these are often for sale as souvenirs: or illustrations of these objects, and a button from a favourite dress or similar

Introduction

Ask the pupils how good their memories are: how well can they remember things? Play a simple version of Kim's Game: show them what is on the tray, allow them several minutes to study and memorize the objects, and then remove one secretly under cover of the cloth. Take the cloth away and see who can be first to identify the missing object. Repeat two or three times.

Sometimes, people need help to remember things they have to do in the future. Some people tie a knot in their handkerchief (demonstrate) to remind them that they must do something. Others use sticky notes: show the pupils these, writing a reminder for yourself on one of them and attaching it to the wall. Ask them if they know any other ways in which people remind themselves about things, such as diaries and calendars.

But sometimes people want to be reminded about something that happened in the past. Some things are so important that they never want to forget them. People might collect things that will remind them of the place they visited or a special event. Show the pupils the souvenirs in turn, either telling them the story behind each, or inventing one for each object. Ask if any of them collect such things. Some of them might collect bookmarks, or postcards, for instance – and what about shells from the beach?

These objects are called souvenirs. This is a French word and means to bring something into your mind – to make you think about something. For instance, a seashell might make us remember a day spent on the beach. It is lovely to look at the shells in the winter and to think again about the holiday, about what it felt like to be collecting the shells.

If you were able to collect some lacemaking equipment, show it to the pupils now, explaining that all lace used to be made by hand using a pillow and bobbins. Some people still make lace this way. Explain that the bobbins need to be weighted at the end, so that they lie flat and steady on the pillow. Beads are used to do this – show them the bobbins. Now, as they did in the past, lacemakers use these bobbins to remind them of events and people. They collect beads from different places or people, or use things such as buttons from special or favourite clothes like wedding dresses or baby clothes. They put these on the bobbins so while they work they are always reminded of happy memories.

PRAYER

Thank you, God, that we can remember things. Thank you that we can think again about happy and exciting times.

REFLECTION

Ask the pupils to look at one of the objects you brought in which reminds them of a happy time. Ask them to think quietly about that time, and then to imagine what it would be like if they could not remember anything about it. Use a prearranged word or sound to show them when the quiet time has ended – or quietly play the first verse of a song.

Note

The pupils could be invited to bring in a souvenir to add to a display about memories. Some of them might like to draw or paint a picture of the experience it recalls. Remind them that a souvenir can be of any event or any day.

8 | Memories 2

You will need

- examples of souvenirs
- suitable musical instruments, possibly school-made ones (but see note at end of Introduction)
- a sheet of paper
- felt-tips

Note

This assembly develops ideas introduced in the previous assembly – 'Memories 1'.

Introduction

Reintroduce the idea of souvenirs: show some examples or invite pupils to do so, and discuss the memories they bring back. These are souvenirs we *look* at, but sometimes, we are reminded of places and events by things we *hear*. When we hear a certain song, we might remember listening to it at a party or singing it at school. There is a story in the Bible about a woman called Deborah who would be reminded of a very important day whenever she heard the sound of rain. The sound would also remind her of what God had done to help her and her people on that day.

Invite some pupils to come and make rain sounds with the instruments. Can they think of a way to improve the sound? Encourage them to think about how they are going to start and finish the rain. When they are satisfied with the sounds, explain that you are going to tell the story of the woman and the rain, and they and the others must listen carefully and decide where the sound of the rain should go. They need not add it on this first reading. You will read the story again afterwards, and they can add it then. (If musical instruments are not available or are inappropriate to the assembly situation, the pupils could experiment with using their fingers or the palms of their hands, on the floor, on their knees, etc.)

Deborah was a very important woman in Israel. She taught the people about God, and she helped them to sort out any problems they had. The people had a big problem at that time. Enemies were attacking their country yet again – and they were very strong enemies. They had a large army and nine hundred chariots. The people of Israel had no proper army and no chariots. When they fought this enemy, they always lost because they could not escape from the chariots or catch up with them. But this time, God promised Deborah that the Israelites would win.

She hurried to Barak, who was Israel's war leader, and told him what God had said. But Barak was afraid. 'We always lose!' he said. 'I will only lead the soldiers if you come with us as well.' So Deborah agreed to go. They marched to a valley nearby and there, on the far side, the enemy was waiting to attack them. Both armies marched into the valley. Barak looked nervously at all the chariots of the enemy. Surely his little army could not win!

But then it started to rain – just a few drops at first, and then a shower. Then more and more rain fell until it was pouring down. It poured onto the enemy, and onto the Israelites and into the river in the valley until the river overflowed its banks. The rain poured onto the ground, and the ground became wetter and wetter. It became so wet that the chariots began to go more and more slowly as their wheels sank into the mud, until the horses could not move the chariots at all. The soldiers in the chariots could not escape, and the Israelites defeated them easily.

Note

Pause at the appropriate stages in the story to allow for the sound effects.

PRAYER

Ask the pupils (or some of them) to make the rain sound at the beginning of each line of the prayer, while your hand is raised:

(rain sounds)
reminded Deborah of the day of battle.
(rain sounds)
reminded her of her small army and frightened leader.
(rain sounds)
reminded her of the enemy's soldiers and chariots.
BUT
(rain sounds)
also reminded her that God helped them to win.

REFLECTION

The enemy panicked without their chariots. Barak did not feel brave without Deborah. Ask the pupils to think about what makes them feel brave. Can they help others to be brave?

9 Memories 3

You will need

- enlarged photocopies of the drawings of Paul's souvenirs on pages 114 and 115, each picture on a separate sheet

Introduction

(If necessary, begin with the introduction about souvenirs on page 20.)

Today, we are going to learn about a person whose souvenirs might have included these things – ask pupils to hold up each picture in turn, describing what each one is as necessary. Ask the others to put up their hands when they think they know what the person might have done during his life. Comment on their ideas as you work, pointing out that this man did several different jobs, so some of the suggestions are correct – but each one for only part of his life.

The person was actually a man called Paul. He lived a long time ago, at about the same time as Jesus. He lived a very dangerous and exciting life. All of these things would have reminded him of different parts of his life. Ask the pupils how many things there are. Ask them to look at the pictures while you tell the story. They must listen carefully: when one of these things is mentioned, they must – secretly – keep a tally on their fingers. One of the things will not be mentioned. How many of them will be able to tell you what it is at the end?

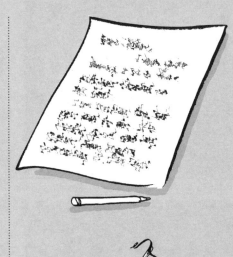

Paul was a very clever and important man. At first, he tried to get rid of all the Christians, but then he became a friend of Jesus too. Then he knew that he must travel round telling people about Jesus and about God's love for them. He was often in great danger when he did this. Other people tried to stop him. They whipped him and threw him into prison. He was often hungry and tired. Sometimes, he managed to do some work to buy food. He was a tent-maker, and spent time sewing tents with some of the many friends he found as he travelled.

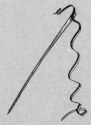

But his enemies would not let him escape. He was arrested, and taken on a long and dangerous journey to Rome to be put on trial in front of the Roman Emperor. On the way, the boat he was in was wrecked in a storm. Then, after Paul and the men with him had struggled to land, a snake bit him! But God kept him safe through all these dangers. When he finally arrived in Rome, he was kept a prisoner in a house, chained to a soldier. But even after all of this, he still told other people that knowing God loved him was the most important thing of all.

Ask what was missing (the page of writing): explain that, when Paul was a prisoner, he still wanted to tell people about Jesus and about how Jesus wanted them to live. The only way Paul could do this was to write letters to them. Christians still read these letters today.

REFLECTION

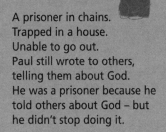

Ask the pupils to watch you. Sit down, and write on a sheet of paper while you read the reflection:

> A prisoner in chains.
> Trapped in a house.
> Unable to go out.
> Paul still wrote to others, telling them about God.
> He was a prisoner because he told others about God – but he didn't stop doing it.

10 Poppies

You will need

- a Remembrance poppy (more if you wish to make a display)

Introduction

Andrew was getting ready for bed. His father came into his bedroom. 'Here you are,' he said, 'I've got your clean socks here. I'll put them away for you.' He opened the drawer, and saw a small stone. 'What's this doing in here? I don't know! Your drawers are always a mess, even when I bring your clothes up for you!'

Andrew took the stone from his father. 'I'm sorry, Dad,' he said, 'but I want to keep it there, where I will see it every morning. You see, it's to remind me of something.'

'What can a stone remind you of, Andrew?' his father said angrily.

'Remember last week, when I was so angry with you that I threw a stone – and broke the kitchen window?'

'Yes! I remember how upset *I* was, too!' his father said grimly.

'Well, this is to remind me about how everyone felt, just because I lost my temper. When I see it in the morning, it reminds me of last week, and it reminds me to try to keep calm. I thought it was a good idea, Dad.'

His father didn't say anything for a few moments, and then he said, 'Yes, I think it's a good idea too, Andrew – a very good idea. I think I need something to put in my drawer to remind me to listen before I get annoyed!'

Recap or introduce the idea of souvenirs (see page 20).

Usually, we keep souvenirs to remind us of happy times. But sometimes we decide we need to be reminded about sad things or about things which were wrong and which hurt people. People hope that if they remember these things, they will not do wrong things again, because they will think about how unhappy people were at the time.

At this time of year, many people are thinking about things that happened in the past. Over eighty years ago, most of the countries in Europe were fighting in the First World War. About thirty years later, many countries were fighting in the Second World War. In the years in between and in the years since then, men and women from many countries have fought in many different wars. All over the world today, there are people who have fought in wars, or who remember people they loved who fought in wars. Every year in this country, people can buy poppies like this one. They are to remind people of the great bravery of all the women and men who fought in and lived through the wars. Many of these were killed or injured. The lives of many other people were ruined by the wars, too.

At the same time, people do not just *think* about the people who have suffered. The money raised from selling these poppies is used to help people who have been injured in war, or people whose loved ones died in war. Poppies were chosen because a man who wrote poems once saw one of the battlefields of the First World War after the battle had ended, and it was covered with poppies. He thought that poppies would remind people of the battlefields.

REFLECTION

A display of poppies could be made for the pupils to look at while they think about the people who bravely fought in the wars.

LINK

This Time of Year section, pages 8–19

11 Do Your Sums!

You will need

- ten sheets of A4 paper numbered 1 to 10, with the corresponding Mayan number on the back of each (see opposite).
- an A4 sheet with the + symbol on it
- an A4 sheet with the = symbol on it
- a map or globe

Introduction

We are going to do some maths! Give out the ten number sheets, in random order, to some of the younger pupils to hold up with the Arabic numerals showing. Ask them or other younger pupils to put them into order. This is how we write our numbers 1 to 10, and many other countries use these numbers too. But once, more countries had different ways of writing numbers – which made life very confusing for travellers! Over a thousand years ago, some people called the Mayans wrote their numbers like this: turn over the sheets for 1 to 5 in turn, with the pupils continuing to hold them up. When you arrive at 6, before turning it over, ask if they can guess how this number was written. Show them how it was written, and make sure they all understand how the system of numbering works. Then arrange the pupils holding the sheets to produce simple sums using the + and = symbol sheets, for example:

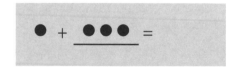

Ask the older pupils to work these out. You could then ask some of them to come out and produce other sums for you or the pupils to do. Remind them that they must say whether the answer is right or not. Thank your helpers and ask them to sit down.

The Mayans lived in the country we now call Guatemala, in Central America. (Show the pupils where this is, relating it to other countries they already know.) They were very wealthy people. They lived in great stone-built cities, and many people still travel to see the ruins of these today. They were very clever builders, and they led comfortable lives, growing good crops.

But now things are very different for their descendants. (Explain this word, if necessary.) Most of them are very poor. There has been civil war in their country for a long time, with one group of people fighting another group. Many families leave their farms and come to live in the cities. But when they arrive there, they find there are not enough jobs for them. Many have to make homes for themselves out of cardboard and plastic sheets. Many cannot afford to look after their children. Some of the children have to work hard every day. Other children have no jobs and nowhere to live except on the streets. But now there are new places for these children to live. In the next assembly, we will hear more about the children and about the people who work hard to help them.

Mayan Numbers

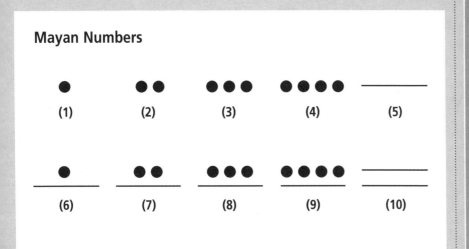

| (1) | (2) | (3) | (4) | (5) |

| (6) | (7) | (8) | (9) | (10) |

REFLECTION

Hold up one of the Mayan number sheets. Ask the pupils to look at this and to think about what you are saying:

The children who used these numbers a thousand years ago were children just like you, even though they lived in a different country at a different time.
The children in that country now who have nowhere to live are children just like you.
Think about the ways in which they are like you.

12 Children's Games

You will need

- (if possible) examples of 'old' games (see below) or pictures of some of them

Introduction

Ask the pupils what games are being played in the school playground at the moment. Perhaps some pupils could demonstrate suitable ones. Ask if they ever pretend to be someone else in any of their games – someone from a story or television programme or a real person.

Once, you could tell what time of the year it was by the games being played in the schools' playgrounds. Children still play some of the games from years ago, such as hopscotch, marbles, and skipping. Can any of the pupils demonstrate these? Other games, like whip and top, ball and cup, and hoop and stick, have almost disappeared. Demonstrate any of these you can, or show pictures of them.

Remind the pupils what they learned in the last assembly about children in Guatemala today, or introduce this information now (see page 29).

In the early 1990s, two people in Britain were watching television. They were called Duncan and Jenni Dyason. They saw a programme about these children who were living on the streets. They learned how difficult and lonely the children's lives were. They saw that the children had very few toys or time to play with them. The children had to do any work they could find to earn some food. Duncan and Jenni lived in a comfortable house with their small daughter, but they knew straight away that they must do something to help the children in Guatemala. They and their daughter went to live there. At first, the children did not trust Duncan and Jenni, but, very slowly, they realized that these two people really did want to help them, and that they loved them, whatever they had done in the past.

Now, there are more people working to help the children, and they are called 'The Toybox Charity'. They go out into the streets in teams called – of course! – 'Street Teams'. They look for children who need their help. There are now several buildings where these children can go for good food, shelter and love.

One day, one of the helpers called Rachel saw a group of street children playing a game she had never seen before. She watched them for a while, and then asked them what the game was about. They told her that it was called 'The Street Team'. The children each pretend to be one of the people who come to help them in the Street Teams. Then they pretend to do whatever that person does – first aid, talking to the children, or bringing them food.

These children in Guatemala are not pretending to be anyone famous. They are pretending to be someone who is very important to them. The workers for Toy Box are changing the lives of these children.

REFLECTION

Ask the pupils to think for a few minutes about what their lives would be like if they had no toys, no safe space in which to play, and no time to play. Ask them to think also about their favourite toy or game. Then read this reflection to close:

Every child needs to play. Every child needs toys and games. Every child needs space and time. Not every child has these things. But there are many people helping them. How do we feel about sharing our games and toys?

Note

Schools can send for more information from: The Toybox Charity, P. O. Box 660, Amersham, Bucks, HP6 6EA. Primary schools can ask to be sent the *Toybox Times* each term.

13 Our Dream Village

Note

The assembly can focus on a dream village, town or city, as appropriate.

You will need

- 2 large sheets of paper
- felt-tips
- a globe (preferably) or a world map

Introduction

There are sometimes advertisements on television or in the papers for 'dream holidays'. Discuss what this means with the pupils. Today, we are going to design 'Our Dream Village' (see note above) on this sheet of paper. Ask the pupils to think quietly for a few moments about what they would like to have in their dream or ideal village. Listen to and comment on their ideas, drawing the popular suggestions on one of the sheets of paper or inviting pupils to do so. When finished, talk about which of the suggestions are for 'luxury' additions, and which are for 'necessities'. Ask which buildings etc. the village could not manage without. Did they include any of these?

Our Dream Village

A few years ago, a group of people sat down together to design their 'Dream Village' on a 'Dream Map'. But the village they wanted was very different from the village the pupils would like to have. These people lived in a small village in India (show them India on the globe or map). The village was called Derinaju, and these are some of the things the villagers wanted. (As you name and explain each one, draw it on the second sheet of paper or invite pupils to do so.)

- a shop – their village did not have a shop
- a well giving clean water – their village did not have clean water
- a new bridge – the old one was not safe
- compost tips – where rubbish could be kept safely; before, they had to dump rubbish at the end of the village where children might play
- electricity – their village had none
- toilets – they did not have any hygienic toilets

Discuss how these are all things which we take for granted. The village did not have many of the things we think we could not live without. Four years after they made their 'Dream Map', the villagers had managed to get all of these things for their village. They had worked very hard and helped each other, and they had been helped by people working for a Christian charity called World Vision.

World Vision believes that God loves people who are poor just as much as he loves richer people, and that Jesus wants them to help these people all over the world. World Vision does not just send money to people in need and tell them what to do to make their home and their village better places in which to live. Instead, workers from World Vision get to know the villagers, and help them to decide what they want – just as in Derinaju in India, where World Vision helped the people to build their own well.

PRAYER

Help us, Lord, to see what people really need. Help us to be good listeners as well as doers. Help us to think about the many things we take for granted each day, and to say thank you for them.

14 Raindrops

Note

Some preparation is needed for this assembly. The pupils need to experience being out in the rain: it would obviously not be a good idea to take them out deliberately in the rain, so the teacher could take the opportunity to prepare them for this assembly on an afternoon when they are going to have to go home in the rain in any case. Explain to them that you are going to do an assembly about being in the rain. Ask them to think about what it feels like to be out in the rain – on foot or in a car or bus – as they go home tonight. Ask them to try to remember all of this for the next day (or whenever)! (This could be used as a class assembly, rather than with the whole school.)

You will need

- a large sheet of paper
- felt-tips
- a tray of rich damp soil or potting compost
- rubber or disposable gloves for the teacher to wear
- a tray of clean, safe sand

Introduction

Remind the pupils about their journey home in the rain. Ask for their memories of what it felt like. Collect any appropriate words or feelings down one side of the sheet of paper. Allow them considerable freedom here. They can use words to describe the rain itself, what the rain felt like, what they felt like when they were out in the rain. Ask how many of them ever complain about the rain. Has the rain spoiled any outings or events for them lately? Thinking about times such as these, can they add any more words to their list?

Raindrops

Explain that you are going to ask them to use their imaginations to help them give you another list of words about rain. Show them the soil, using the gloves. Mould it to show that it is damp. Ask if they think plants could grow in it. Then show them the sand, letting some trickle through your fingers as you speak, telling them how dry it is. Could any plants grow in this?

Ask them to close their eyes and to imagine this: they are living in a very hot country, miles away from here. Their families are farmers, growing all their own food. If they don't grow enough food, they cannot get any from anywhere else: there are no shops. It is very hot today. They are sitting outside their homes, looking at their fields. The fields are brown and dry. There is no green plant anywhere in sight. It has not rained here for seven whole months. They know that there is not much food left. Suddenly, they feel something on their heads. They hold out their hands – and they are wet! It is raining! It is pouring! The dry soil round them becomes darker and wetter and turns into mud. Now, the seeds will grow and their family will have fruit and vegetables to eat.

Ask the pupils to open their eyes. If they were the children in that story, what words would they use to describe the rain and how it made them feel? Collect these words on the second half of the sheet of paper.

PRAYER

Ask the pupils to watch the sand trickling through your fingers as you read the prayer:

God, thank you for rain. We often complain about it because we seem to get too much of it at the wrong times. Help us to remember that we need rain, and to see that it can be beautiful.

Note

Some pupils might like to follow this up with writing simple poems, individually or as a class, from two points of view. One could be by a child who has missed a trip to the seaside because of the rain. The other could be by a child in the story about rain. How would each of these describe rain? They could begin 'I hate rain!' and 'I love rain!'

15 Have You Got Any Water?

You will need

- a clear jug of clean water
- a bowl

Introduction

Today's assembly is about something we all tend to take for granted. It is something we all have to use every day. It has no colour – unless it is dirty! Very often, we deliberately make it dirty. Other times, we make it dirty by accident. Without it, we would soon be dirty ourselves. Worse than that, we would be very thirsty! It is water. (If the assembly on page 32, about the villagers' dream of having clean water, has been presented, refer to this now.)

Most of us in this country have only to turn on a tap to have as much clean, fresh water as we want. Ask the pupils to think about what we use water for each day. Ask some of them to come out and mime a use of water for the others to guess. If the following are not included, whisper each to a pupil, and ask them to mime it for you: drinking; washing ourselves, our clothes, our pots and pans, and our houses; flushing the toilet.

Discuss with them how important water is for all these things, and how its use protects us from illness and disease. Ask what life would be like without water. What about life in school? Do they think life in school would be healthy and pleasant without water? Discuss what each of these groups of people would not be able to do: the pupils themselves; teachers and classroom helpers; kitchen staff; caretakers. What could everyone do if the school had no water supply?

Core material

Many schools in other parts of the world do not have clean water. A few years ago, there was a school like this in the village of Mankote in the Himalaya Mountains in India. The only water for the teachers and pupils to use each day came from a water-hole (a spring) hundreds of metres away. The caretaker had to carry the water to the school. It wasn't very clean because animals used the water-hole, too. The children and their parents were often ill because of the dirty water.

Then a group of people – the Kassar Trust – showed the villagers how to bring clean water up from a stream that ran underground. Another group of people, Christian Aid, gave the villagers the money they needed to buy equipment to do this. Then the villagers started work. They had to dig through solid rock to reach the stream. Then they had to dig trenches for the pipes which would carry the water. The pupils all helped with this as much as they could. Now, the school has a water supply. It is pumped by hand, and the water runs through the pipes into a covered tank at the school. Fewer pupils are ill now, because their water is clean.

REFLECTION

Ask the pupils to watch and think while you slowly pour the water into the bowl as you read these lines:

Clean, fresh water.
So simple: it's always there for us.
Washing, drinking, swimming.
Always plenty of water for us to use.
Next time you drink some water, or flush the toilet, or put on fresh, clean clothes, remember that not everyone can do that.

16 How Much Water Do You Need?

You will need

- two 1-litre jugs, a litre of water in one
- a large, clean empty bucket or bowl
- a sheet of paper and felt-tips

Introduction

Talk about the uses of water mentioned in the last assembly, reminding pupils of the importance of each one. These are the ways in which we use water.

Now ask pupils if they know how much water we use in a day. We are going to think about four uses of water – filling the kettle, washing up pots and pans, flushing the toilet, and using the washing-machine. On the sheet of paper, draw a kettle, a washing-up bowl, a toilet and a washing-machine. Show the pupils what a litre of water looks like by pouring it from one jug into the other over the bucket or bowl. Give them a few minutes to estimate each amount, and then ask them how much water they think each of these uses would take. Listen to their suggestions. Then write these average amounts next to the pictures: kettle – 1 litre; washing up – 8 litres; flushing the toilet – 7 litres; washing-machine – 95 litres.

Doing all of these things is very easy for us: we just turn on the tap, pull the chain or push the handle, or switch on the machine. In many countries, getting water is not that easy! Awa is a young girl who lives with her family in a village in Senegal in West Africa. They have no taps in their house. They do not even have a tap in the village! They used to get their water from the village pond, but that water was dirty, and they were often ill. Now, Awa and her mother use a well that has been built. Its water is clean – but it is three miles away! Ask the pupils how far Awa has to walk altogether to fetch water.

As well as walking so far, Awa and her mother have to carry the water home, and it is very heavy. Ask one of the pupils to lift up the full litre jug. Awa can carry about 8 litres. Her mother carries about fifteen. Ask how they think the water is carried. In fact, Awa and her mother carry the water in buckets balanced on their heads. If Awa had to fetch enough water for a washing-machine to be used once, she would have to go to the well twelve times! She can carry 8 litres: how much water would be left in her bucket after we had flushed one of our toilets just once?

Awa and her family do not have flush toilets or washing-machines. But the family does need a lot of water. Everybody in the world needs at least 5 litres of water a day just to stay alive. But everybody needs 30 litres a day to stay healthy and clean. Awa has a brother. So there are three of them in the family. If Awa and her mother go all the way to the well and back once a day, they bring enough water for the three of them to drink, but only a very little water for washing and cooking. A family in our country uses about sixty bucketfuls of water a day!

REFLECTION

Pour the water slowly from jug to jug while you speak, asking the pupils to watch the water.

Water!
Turn on a tap – or walk three miles!
Water!
Need a drink? Walk three miles, then three miles back carrying the water.
Water!
Need a bath? Sorry – there's no water left.

17 Operation Christmas Child

You will need

- two boxes wrapped as Christmas presents – one much larger than the other
- an empty shoebox
- examples of small presents that would fit into the shoebox, such as pencils, notebooks, small toy car, small doll, crayons, toothbrush, etc.
- an enlarged Operation Christmas Child logo – see page 116.

Introduction

If this assembly is being used in the run-up to Christmas, talk about looking forward to presents, the excitement of seeing presents on Christmas Day, and trying to guess what they are from their size and shape. Show the pupils the two parcels, and ask who would prefer to have the bigger one. Talk about the size of a present not always being a reflection of its value: jewellery usually comes in small parcels, but it is often worth much more than many larger presents. One present can often be worth more than another present in other ways too. Talk about the non-monetary value of objects, by referring to the value of a present made by a child for their parent. To the parent, this can be worth far more than an expensive present from someone else.

In 1996, over one million children all over the world were given just one present – one of these (show them the shoebox). For many of them, this was the first present they had ever been given. Each child had just one box, but when they opened it, they found out that it was full of lots of little presents! One child was so amazed to be given so many presents that he thought he had to choose just one of them, and he tried to give the others back to the adult who had given him the box! Some of the children who received the boxes were ill or had no family to live with. Others had lost their homes through war or floods.

These shoeboxes were filled with presents by lots of different people. Many of them were children, the same ages as the children who received the boxes. They were all helping a charity called Operation Christmas Child, which tries to take as many presents as it can to children all over the world who would not get any other presents. Children decide what to put into the boxes, and many shops and firms help too. They give things, like chocolate, to go into the box, or they help the charity to collect the boxes and to take them wherever they need to go. Some firms give the boxes themselves for others to fill! Other things are needed too. In 1996, the charity used 150 miles of tape to fasten up all the boxes!

What sorts of things can the pupils think of that would fit into a shoebox and would be good presents for children who have very little of their own? Take their suggestions, commenting on their suitability as you go, trying to point out to the pupils that these children are in need of many basic things we take for granted. Invite some pupils to come and pack a shoebox for a child, using the presents provided.

Make sure that the pupils understand that they should not feel guilty if they have the things they need and lots of presents at Christmas. Point out that they can make sure they say thank you for these things, and that they do not forget that other people might not have as much as they have.

(*Note:* Pupils should never be left with a feeling of guilt.)

REFLECTION

Look at the logo for Operation Christmas Child. What is it? Can the pupils think why this design was chosen? Ask them to look at it while you read the following:

Just a shoebox.
Not very big, and very ordinary.
But inside are presents chosen and packed with love.
Each one is special to the child who gets it.
Think – what would you put in the box for a child like you?

Note

Some schools might like to investigate how their pupils could take part in filling shoeboxes. The address for further information is:

Samaritan's Purse International / Operation Christmas Child, Victoria House, Victoria Road, Buckhurst Hill, Essex, IG9 5EX.

18 Listen Carefully!

Note

It will be easier in some schools to use this as a class assembly, rather than a whole-school assembly. Ensure the pupils are aware of your school's usual safety rules for being outside. If it is impractical to do the assembly at all in this format, a version can easily be done in which the pupils complete the listening exercise in their places in assembly. If your school is in a very noisy area, you might prefer to take the pupils to another room in the school, or just to use their classroom.

You will need

- (if possible) a one-minute timer or a stopwatch
- a piece of paper and a pencil for each child or just for the teacher, as appropriate

Note

In this series of assemblies on 'Hearing', sensitivity needs to be exercised if there is a pupil or an adult with hearing impairment in the group or school. Individual teachers who know the person concerned will be best able to judge which parts – if any – of these assemblies should be used.

Outdoors

As soon as the pupils are outside, ask them what they can hear. When they have told you the obvious things, tell them that you are sure there are other sounds they are not hearing. Ask them to stand (or sit if possible) so that they are not disturbing anyone else. Ask them to put their paper and pencil (if used) on the ground, to fold their arms and to close their eyes. They must stay as quiet as possible for one minute, when the timer will go off. During this time, they must listen as hard as they can, and remember anything they hear. Tell them when you are setting the timer, and then listen with them.

When the timer goes off, ask them to remain quiet as they pick up their paper, and write down all they heard, or younger pupils could draw some of the things. Alternatively, they can tell you what they heard. If they are still motivated, repeat the exercise to see if they can add anything.

Indoors

Take the pupils back into school. Compare the lists. Did they hear many things they had missed at first? Ask them to think about how important it is to be able to hear clearly and well. If they do not raise such issues, ask them to consider emergency situations and conversations with other people. Ask them to think about what they would miss hearing and what they will need to hear in the next day or days.

PRAYER

Scraping chairs and banging doors,
Rustling paper and scrunchy crisps,
Whispered secrets, shouted cheers,
Singing birds and barking dogs –
Thank you, God, for all of these.

19 What Can You Hear?

Note

This assembly builds on listening activities in the previous assembly – 'Listen Carefully!'. It does require preparation of a tape: but once made, it can be used again with different groups.

You will need

- a tape-recording of various sounds: home-based (television, vacuum cleaner, washing-machine, baby crying, food mixer, telephone, doorbell, etc.) or school-based (pages turning, books closing, music, a P.E. lesson, a computer in use, one or two identifiable staff voices, dinner-time, construction 'bricks' being sorted through, the bell, etc.). Record these with breaks in between, so you can stop the tape while you ask pupils what each sound was. The tape should start with a sound that is easy to identify. Ensure that each sound lasts long enough for pupils to be able to recognize it.
- a tape-recorder
- paper and pen for your own record of points

Introduction

Refer to the assembly on page 42 in which the pupils had to listen very carefully. Say that you are now going to test those 'listening' skills. Explain that you are going to play some mystery sounds to them one at a time, and that after each one you will ask them what the sound was. Tell them whether the sounds are those they might hear at school or at home. Ask them to sit as quietly as they can so that everyone can listen.

Play through the tape, awarding them a point for each sound they identify and giving yourself a point for each one they do not identify. You might like to say that you will accept only three guesses for each one, else they might want to carry on guessing.

We now know what all of those mystery sounds were. Our ears can identify lots of different sounds. Talk about telephone calls and being able to tell who is speaking on the other end of the line before they say their name. New-born babies already know the voices of their mother and sometimes of their elder brothers and sisters!

As well as being able to identify different voices, our ears can often tell how the person is feeling from the sound of their voice. Show the pupils what you mean by saying the phrase 'Class two, come over here' in several different ways – as if you were annoyed with them, as if you were very pleased with them, and as if you were frightened. Talk about the different sound of your voice each time. If time permits, you can then ask some pupils to say another phrase (such as 'It's time to go home') as if they felt tired, happy, surprised, angry, sad, etc.

Our ears are very clever!

PRAYER

Explain that you are going to list some of the things our ears can do, and invite them to join in if they wish with the 'thank you' you are going to add after each one.

Our ears can recognize a friendly voice – thank you, God.
Our ears can tell when someone is sad – thank you, God.
Our ears can tell us what is happening – thank you, God.
Our ears can hear danger signals – thank you, God.
Our ears can hear someone telling us they love us – thank you, God.

20 The Boy who Listened

Introduction

Refer to the assembly about mystery sounds (page 44) or talk about identifying mystery sounds now. A mystery sound at night can be frightening! But usually it turns out to be something like the water pipes, our sister, or the cat! There is a story about a mystery sound at night in the Bible, and the person who heard it was a boy called Samuel. Choose pupils to mime the actions of Samuel and Eli while you read the story. The rest of the pupils can join in by saying, 'Samuel!' when they hear the words 'a voice calling ...' or 'the voice again, calling ...'. Practise this now.

Samuel didn't live with his mother and father. They had brought him to live in a special building where people came to worship God. They knew that God wanted Samuel to work for him. They still came to see him, of course, and Samuel didn't live there alone. Several other people lived there too. Their job was to teach the people about God and to help them when they came to worship him there. One of them was called Eli. He was quite an old man, and Samuel was a big help to him. Samuel fetched and carried things for him, and helped him in his work. Sometimes, in the middle of the night, Eli needed a drink, and then he would call for Samuel and he would hurry to help him.

One night, everything was quiet. Eli and Samuel were both asleep in their own rooms. It was dark. Suddenly, Samuel heard a voice calling, 'Samuel!' He sat up quickly, rubbing his eyes, and hurried to Eli.

Eli woke up with a jump. 'What is it, Samuel?' he asked. 'Are you all right?'

Samuel said, '*I'm* all right, Eli! But what do *you* want?'

Eli was puzzled. He told Samuel that he had not called him. He told him to go back to bed. 'You must have been dreaming!' he said.

Samuel snuggled down in bed again. He had had a busy day, and he was soon fast asleep again. But then he heard the voice again, calling, 'Samuel!'

It must be Eli! He rushed back to him – but Eli said, 'No, I didn't call you. Go back to sleep, Samuel!'

Samuel went back to bed, and soon all was quiet again. Then there was the voice again, calling: 'Samuel! Samuel!'

The boy hurried over to Eli. 'This time I'm sure I heard you!' he said. Then Eli realized who was calling Samuel. It was God! 'Go back to bed, Samuel,' he said. 'Next time you hear the voice, say, "I am listening, Lord. What do you want me to do?" Because it is God who is calling you,' he explained.

So Samuel went back to bed yet again, and this time, when he heard his name, he said just what Eli had told him to say.

That was the first time God spoke to Samuel. God spoke to Samuel all through the rest of his life, giving him important messages to pass on to his people. Soon, other people knew that God was speaking to Samuel.

REFLECTION

Ask the pupils to sit quietly and think while you read the reflection:

God trusted Samuel to pass on important messages to other people. Can people trust you to pass on important messages and to do the things they ask you to do? Do you listen when people are trying to tell you something?

21 Listening to Music

You will need

- a recording of one of the pupils' favourite pieces of music
- a keyboard or chime bar if a piano is unavailable. Some teachers may be able to provide different instruments for the pupils to identify, or pictures of them, or recordings – such as Britten's *The Young Person's Guide to the Orchestra.* This section of the assembly can be expanded if required to fit in with any current work on instruments.

Note

This assembly builds on listening activities and ideas introduced in 'Listen Carefully' and 'What Can You Hear?', pages 42 and 44.

Introduction

If possible, play the piece of favourite music as the pupils enter assembly.

We have been thinking about all the different things our ears can do. Another thing that many people enjoy doing with their ears is listening to music. Take a quick poll to find out which singers or groups are the most popular at the moment. Include any adults present in this, pointing out how people's 'musical tastes' differ – explain what the phrase means, likening it to people's preferences for certain foods.

Whatever type of music people enjoy, they can get great pleasure and enjoyment from it. Our ears are doing several important jobs while we relax and listen to our music. If they could talk to us, they could tell us many different facts about the music.

Listening to Music

Our ears can tell us what instruments are playing in a piece of music – although practice is needed here. Play some well-known instruments, or show pictures of or play recordings of them, asking the pupils to tell you what they are. They can then mime the playing of that instrument.

Our ears can tell us which parts of the music are louder than others, or when the music becomes very quiet for some reason. Play the same note on a piano, keyboard or chime bar several times, varying the volume, asking the pupils to raise their hands when the sound is louder.

Our ears can also tell us which notes are higher or lower in pitch than others. (If necessary, play a note from each end of the keyboard, explaining which we refer to as 'high' and which as 'low'.) Play one note, and then play a higher or lower one (at least three tones apart), asking the pupils if its pitch is higher or lower. Repeat this two or three times.

Our ears can tell us when something is played wrongly, too. If possible, play a tune they know well, and make a deliberate mistake in it, asking them to raise their hands when they hear it.

Our ears could tell us lots of other things too. But the main thing they tell us is that music is fun to listen to!

REFLECTION

Music is everywhere:
  in the shops,
  in our rooms,
  in the streets!
  on the television,
  on our tapes,
  on the bus!
  at school,
  at home –
  everywhere!

PRAYER

The following prayer could then be used, if appropriate.

Thank you, God, for the pleasure music gives to us. Thank you for the many people who compose it for us and for all of us who can play it.

22 Hearing Dogs

Hearing Dogs

Note

This assembly builds on listening activities and ideas introduced in 'Listen Carefully!', 'Listening to Music' and 'What Can You Hear?', pages 42, 48 and 44.

You will need

- an alarm clock
- a kitchen timer
- various bells from the school's musical instruments
- a large soft toy dog

Introduction

Remind the pupils as necessary about the loud and quiet noises they heard during the assembly on page 48, and the mystery noises they heard during the assembly on page 44. When we listened very carefully (page 42), we could hear a lot of noises. When we listened carefully, we could tell what the mystery noises were.

Note

Further information can be obtained from: Hearing Dogs for the Deaf, The Training Centre, London Road, Lewknor, Oxon, OX9 5RY.

But some people cannot hear noises very clearly no matter how hard they try. They cannot hear as clearly as most of us can, because there is something damaged in their ears. No matter how hard they try, many noises are mystery noises to them, and they cannot tell what they are or what people are saying. Some people cannot hear any noises at all. Some people are helped by wearing hearing-aids. (Explain their use to the pupils.) And some of them now have something else to help them – something hairy and alive!

Core material

We are all used to seeing guide dogs helping people who cannot see to walk through busy streets safely. Some people who cannot hear well now have 'hearing dogs' living with them. Ask the pupils what they think these dogs do.

Ask them to think about a deaf person, who cannot hear at all, living at home alone or at work. Set the kitchen timer to go off immediately. What might this be telling people? Talk about the use of timers. Ask a pupil to come out and hold the kitchen timer. Show them how to set it off. What other bells are used in a house or office or school? Take suggestions and comment on them: give clues if necessary to such things as the door-bell, telephone-bell, fire-bell, smoke alarms, baby alarms, alarm clocks. Discuss why people need to know about all of these – for communication *and* safety reasons. Give out bells to pupils to represent each of the suggested bells. Ask what happens when one of these bells goes off: would a deaf person be able to hear any of them? Would they need to hear them?

Hearing dogs are trained to tell their owners when any of these bells or alarms go off. Ask the pupils for suggestions on how the dogs do this, pointing out that barking is useless. The dogs are trained to touch their owners with their paws to tell them a bell or alarm is going off. When they have the person's attention, they lead them to the bell. Tell the pupils that you are going to ask another adult to take the part of the deaf person, and that you are going to play the part of the dog with the toy dog! Ask the pupil holding the kitchen timer to set it off. Demonstrate what the dog would do. Do the same for the telephone or another 'non-emergency' bell, asking the pupils to ring their bells to represent the real ones. But what if the bell is warning of danger, such as a fire-bell? Then, the dog lies down after touching its owner. The owner then knows that there is danger. Demonstrate what happens with an emergency bell and the dog.

It takes a long time to train a hearing dog. First they must learn how to behave in company and in a house, so that they are not a nuisance to their owner and will do their work properly. Then they have another four months' training, learning what all the bells and alarms in their new owner's home sound like. The dog's owner comes to stay with the dog, so that they can get used to each other, then the training continues at the owner's home.

While they are being trained, the dogs wear a special jacket. Once they are fully trained, this jacket is replaced by one that has the words 'Hearing Dogs for the Deaf' on it. Everyone can then see that this is a very special dog! As well as all the help the dogs give to their owners, they also bring them love and companionship, just as other dogs do.

REFLECTION

Next time you hear any sort of bell, remember the Hearing Dogs, and think what it would be like if you could not hear that bell.

or

It is very easy to become annoyed with people when they can't hear us clearly. Encourage the pupils to think about how they can help people, instead of making things more difficult for them.

PRAYER

God, help us always to remember to look after animals. Thank you for the animals who work hard for us. Thank you for the dogs who are clever enough to learn how to be Hearing Dogs, and who want to help people like this.

23 A Good Story

Introduction

Ask how many of the pupils enjoy listening to stories. Invite some to tell you the name of their favourite story: encourage them to say why they like that particular story. Discuss what makes a story a 'good story' – for instance, excitement, the characters, action, danger, description, etc. Alternatively, some pupils might like to read their own stories to the others.

Sometimes, stories can teach us something in a way that is easy to understand. (Perhaps you could think of an example here from a school favourite.) We can enjoy the story and be learning about something at the same time. Sometimes it is easy to work out what the story is telling us. Ask the pupils to listen to this story, and to think about what it is saying.

There was once a black and white dog who was very greedy. One day, he was watching as his owner cooked her dinner. The food smelt very good! She had just put a lovely pork chop on a plate when the telephone rang. She hurried into the other room to answer it. Quick as a flash, the dog put his front legs on the table – and grabbed the meat in his teeth! Then he ran out into the garden and through the fence into the field. He thought, 'I'll go into the trees over there. No one will see me there!'

He had to cross a bridge over a stream to get to the trees. As he crossed it, he looked down at the water – and there was another dog, with a chop in his mouth! 'Look at that!' he thought. 'If I take that meat off him, I'll have two chops to eat instead of just one!'

So he growled at the other dog to frighten him. But the other dog didn't drop the meat. 'I'll bark at him – that will make him drop it!' he thought. As soon as he opened his mouth to bark, the meat fell out of his mouth into the water – and sank! The ripples spread out over the water, and the dog realized that he had been looking at his own reflection all the time.

(Adapted from a fable by Aesop)

Discuss with the pupils why the dogs lost his meat (greed). This story was quite easy to understand. But sometimes it is harder to understand what a story is telling us. And the story must be interesting else we won't be bother reading or listening to it at all. In the next few assemblies, we are going to hear some of the stories Jesus told. Jesus wanted to teach people about God and his love for them. He wanted them to learn how to live as God wanted them to. Sometimes, he used stories to help them to understand what he was saying. These special stories were called parables. The first one we will hear is about a very dangerous journey.

PRAYER

The pupils can be invited to join in the prayer, saying 'Thank you' with you when their own favourite stories/characters are mentioned.

Thank you, God,
  for stories to enjoy:

  for princesses and
  fairies – thank you

  for animals and
  rescues – thank you

  for adventures and
  dangers – thank you

  for sad scenes and happy
  endings – thank you.

24 The Good Samaritan 1

You will need

- a first-aid kit
- (if possible) a first-aider to demonstrate

Note This assembly develops ideas introduced in the previous assembly.

Introduction

Have any of the pupils been injured lately? If appropriate, invite them to tell the others how people took care of them.

Either: Show the first-aid kit and discuss what is in it. Ask the pupils to mime how they would treat a grazed knee or a cut finger.

Or: If a first-aider is present, ask them to show some pupils how to put someone into the recovery position. The importance of finding adult help should be stressed.

Say that it is important to know what to do straight away. Quick action is needed, and can make all the difference. Today's story is about some people who found an injured man – but only one of them did anything to help.

Core material

Recap on the last assembly about good stories and how stories can teach us something. Remind them about the parables Jesus told. This is one of them.

A man needed to travel from Jerusalem to Jericho. This was a very dangerous journey. The road was very steep and led through stony hills. Everyone knew robbers lived there, hiding behind the rocks, waiting for travellers. They would rush out, knock them unconscious, and steal everything they had. People tried to travel together along that road. But this man, whom we will call Simeon, had to go to Jericho that day, and no one could go with him. So he set off alone. He had to walk, and it was a long way!

As he left Jerusalem, the road became steeper. It was very quiet up there. All he could hear was the wind and the birds as they swooped high above him. He was frightened and wished he was not alone. Then he heard another noise! It sounded like falling stones. He looked up. Was someone watching him? He hurried on – and suddenly there were three men in front of him and another one behind! They attacked him, knocking him to the ground. They took everything he had, and laughed at him. Then they left him on the dusty road, and ran off into the rocks.

Simeon was terrified. What would happen if no one came? He knew he needed someone to look after him. Then he heard footsteps. He was safe! But, instead of stopping to help, the man rushed by him, looking up at the rocks in case the robbers were still there. Simeon was left alone again. The sun was very hot, and Simeon dozed. Then something woke him up – footsteps! A man was coming. Surely this man would help him. But no! He hurried past as quickly as he could. He too thought that he might be attacked if he stopped to help. He thought it was far more important to keep himself safe than to help Simeon!

Simeon began to think he was going to die. He wondered if he was ever going to see his family again. When he heard a donkey's hooves, coming towards him, he did not expect to be helped. He was too weak now even to see who it was. Then he felt someone lifting up his head, and realized there was water at his lips. Someone was telling him not to worry. His scratches and bruises were bandaged, and then he was helped onto the man's donkey. Soon, they were at a house, and the man was asking the owner to look after Simeon until he was well enough to go home. The man gave the owner some coins and said, 'I will pay for anything Simeon needs. If this is not enough, I will pay you next time I come.' It was amazing. This man had risked his own life to help Simeon. What made it even more amazing was that he was from the country of Samaria. Now Simeon was a Jew, and his people hated the people of Samaria – and the people of Samaria hated the Jews! This man had stopped to help his enemy.

REFLECTION

Ask the pupils to think for a few minutes about all the people who help us when we are ill or injured – our families, nurses and doctors, St John's Ambulance, paramedics, etc.

PRAYER

Say the following prayer if appropriate:

Thank you, Father, for all the people who look after us when we are ill or injured. (A sentence could be inserted here about the people who looked after some of the pupils recently.) Thank you that some of us will be able to look after ill people as we grow up.

LINK

This assembly could be used as an introduction to the assemblies about The Toybox Charity (page 30) and Operation Christmas Child (page 40), one of the projects handled by an organization called Samaritan's Purse.

25 The Good Samaritan 2

Recap briefly on the story of the good Samaritan, stressing that it was the traveller's enemy who helped him. One of the laws God had given to his people told them to love their neighbour. (Explain that 'to love' here means to look after and care for, not to love in the romantic sense.) Someone said to Jesus, 'I know I am told to love my neighbour, but can you tell me who my neighbour is? What does this law really mean?' Jesus told this story to show what the answer was.

When the Samaritan found the man, he could have said, 'What a shame! Still, I needn't do anything. After all, he's not even from my country. Someone else can help him.' But he didn't say that. He didn't think about what country the man was from. He just saw he needed help, and he helped him straight away. He decided the man was his neighbour, even though he lived miles away from him.

Jesus was telling the people listening to his story that a neighbour is not just someone who lives near you, someone who likes the same football team as you. A neighbour is someone who needs your help. There have been many people who have acted like this. They heard about people who needed help, and they decided to go and help them even though they did not know these people themselves, and they were very different from them. Often, they carried on helping them even when they were in danger themselves, just as the Samaritan was in danger, or when other people have done their best to stop them.

Here are some people who saw people in need and went to help them, treating them as neighbours to be loved and cared for. Teachers can choose from these to fit in with their school's requirements.

REFLECTION

Ask the pupils to close their eyes and to imagine what it would be like to leave everything they have and everyone they know at home, to go to a different country to help people they have never even met.

The Good Samaritan 2

Florence Nightingale

Have any of the pupils been in hospital, as a patient or a visitor? (Be sensitive here to pupils' experiences.) Talk about the conditions in our hospitals. Discuss why cleanliness is needed, and how this is taken for granted in our hospitals. Once, hospitals were very different. When Florence Nightingale was 34 years old in 1854, Britain began to fight a war called the Crimean War in Turkey. Stories reached Britain about the terrible conditions in the soldiers' hospitals there. There were not enough beds, bedding, food or medicines, and rats shared the rooms with the injured soldiers. Nearly half the soldiers were dying after they reached hospital because they were not being looked after properly there.

Florence and others felt sure these men could have been saved. Florence's family was rich. She lived in a comfortable home, and most people would have thought she had all she needed to be happy. But when she was asked to help the soldiers, she knew she had to do so. Her family did not want her to go and even stopped talking to her, and friends thought she was mad! When she arrived in the hospitals, the doctors did not want her to do anything! She had to struggle all the time to be allowed to help the men. She worked for 20 hours at a time. Finally, people realized she could help – by keeping the hospital clean, by feeding the patients and by encouraging them. Soon, very few soldiers were dying in the hospital, just because she decided to go to help soldiers she did not even know. When she came back to Britain, she started a college for nurses, to train them to work in the same way.

Mary Seacole

Mary was born in 1805 in Jamaica. Many people died there from a disease called cholera, and she worked as a nurse to help them. Then, she heard about the Crimean War and how so many soldiers were dying in the terrible hospitals there (details above). She tried to go to nurse them, but people would not pay her fare just because she was black. So she earned money to pay for her own transport. She worked in the Crimea for three years, setting up a sort of 'hotel' where soldiers could get food and medicines. She went onto the battlefields themselves to help the wounded soldiers. When she did come back to Britain, she ran out of money, but some people had realized how brave she had been, and they raised money for her.

Paul and Rachel

Paul and Rachel Lindoewood used to live in Nottingham. They had always had many friends from other countries, and were interested in other countries, especially the poorer places such as parts of Africa. Paul was running a successful business, and Rachel was working as a children's doctor when they applied to work in Kenya with the Methodist Church. Paul uses a wheelchair and he wanted to help other disabled people to lead full lives – to be able to work, to support their families, have friends and to take part in activities in their own communities, as he could in Britain.

In Kenya, many disabled people are not even able to go to school. Many don't have wheelchairs or other things to help them to travel or to do everyday things. Some are not even allowed to live with their own families. They have to beg to get money for food. Disabled people can do more to help each other if they work together. Paul is now working with other disabled people, and with other people, to help them to accept disabled people, so they see disabled people can work and help others and can lead full lives among them. There are not enough doctors in Kenya, especially in the poorer country areas. Rachel is working in a small church hospital, where she treats and looks after people of all ages. They both saw people needing help, and left home to help them.

LINK

'Children's Games', *Other Children* section, page 30

26 Jesus the Shepherd

You will need

- (if possible) toy tools, e.g. a saw or plane
- a long stick
- some small round stones
- a toy sheep

Introduction

At Christmas, Bible stories are told about Jesus' birth and what happened then. Next, the Bible reports what happened when his parents thought he was lost in Jerusalem when he was about twelve years old (page 95). But the rest of the stories in the Bible about Jesus take place when he is grown up and already working. Ask if any of the pupils know what job he was doing. Show them the tools as a clue, and ask them to mime using some of them. (Mime actions yourself such as sawing if you do not have any toy tools.) Mary's husband, Joseph, was a carpenter: discuss what a carpenter does nowadays. Joseph trained Jesus as a carpenter. But when Jesus was about thirty years old, he knew that it was time for him to start the special work that he had come to do. It was time to start telling people about God and his love for them. It was time to start showing them that God loved them by the way Jesus helped them himself.

So, one day, Jesus told people that he had another job. (Show the pupils the stones, the stick and the lamb.) He told them that he was a shepherd. Perhaps some of the people listening to him thought, 'No he's not! He's a carpenter!' But as they thought about what he was saying and saw what happened to him later on, they realized what he meant.

Being a shepherd was not easy in that country. In fact, it was very dangerous! The shepherds had to live out in the hills with the flocks of sheep. They could not leave the sheep because there were wild animals out there who were just waiting for the chance to eat a nice fat sheep or lamb! The shepherds had to protect the sheep. They used stones like these (show them). They would put one of these into a strip of leather and swirl it through the air, letting go of one end of the leather so that the stone shot out at great speed. The shepherds became very good shots, and were able to hit the wild animals to frighten them away. They also used long, strong sticks like this one (show them) to help them guide the sheep in dangerous places, such as steep hills and rocky valleys. Every day, they had to lead the sheep through the hills until they found a safe place with good, fresh grass for them to eat. Then they had to find fresh, flowing water for them. The shepherds could not relax even then, in case any animals attacked the sheep. At night, they returned to their camp. Here, they had a little field with walls made out of rocks, for the sheep to sleep in. To make sure the sheep were safe, the shepherds would lie down to sleep over the entrance to the field, so no animal could reach the sheep.

So it was not an easy life looking after the sheep. Jesus did not work like this, so why did he say he was a shepherd? The people realized he looked after them as well as a shepherd looked after his sheep. A shepherd knew every one of his sheep, and Jesus knew all about every one of the people. A shepherd risked his life to keep the sheep safe, and Jesus risked his life all the time. He had many enemies, but he would not stop helping and teaching the people.

In the end, Jesus died because he would not stop doing this, but Christians believe that he came back to life because he was God's son. Christians believe Jesus is like a shepherd to them too, because he looks after them.

PRAYER

Long before Jesus was born, one of Israel's kings called David thought God was like a shepherd to him. These are words that David wrote, thinking of himself as both a sheep and a person:

The Lord is my
shepherd, he
will give me
what I need.
He will lead
me to places
where I can
rest ...
He will show me
the way to go,
I need not be afraid of
anything because he will be
with me.

(Psalm 23, paraphrased extract)

LINK

'The Good Shepherd', *Music Assemblies* section, page 106

27 The Lost Sheep

Introduction

Ask the pupils if any of them have ever got lost – perhaps while they were shopping. Discuss what it feels like to be lost – to realize you do not know where the person is who you are meant to be with. What does it feel like to be completely alone in a strange place?

One of the special stories Jesus told was about an animal that got lost – a sheep. The country Jesus lived in was not a safe place for a sheep to go wandering off by itself. There were wild animals around, like wolves and bears and mountain lions. Ask the pupils what would happen if any of these met the sheep! Here is the story Jesus told. (Pupils can mime this as you tell it with a minimum of direction from you.)

Core material

The shepherd was tired. It had been a very long day, and he had walked for miles, leading the sheep. There were one hundred of them, and sometimes it seemed that each one wanted to go a different way! It had taken him so long to find some good grass in a place that was safe for the sheep and the small lambs. At last he had found the right place, and there had been a stream there too. The sheep had soon settled down to drink and graze, but he had kept watch all day. There were steep rocky hills nearby. He had had to keep jumping up and hurrying over to stop the sheep from climbing up there. It was too steep for them, and they might fall. There were thorny bushes between the rocks that would catch hold of their woolly coats and would not let go. And, up in the rocks, he saw a lion hiding, waiting for a lamb to wander too close. The shepherd had soon scared him away, but he couldn't relax all day in case he came back.

LINK

'The Good Shepherd', *Music Assemblies* section, page 106

Now, at last, he was on his way home. He plodded on wearily, sometimes calling out to the sheep to remind them they were safe and that he was still there. When he arrived at his camp, the sheep quickly trotted into the field. They were tired, too. He stood at the entrance, counting them as he did each evening. 29, 30 ... he thought of the hot stew he would soon cook ... 56, 57, 58 ... he was very hungry! 82, 83 ... he was tired, too, ready for bed ... 98, 99 ... That was it! No more sheep were coming. One was missing! He knew which one it was! It was the ewe with the floppy ear – the one who was always wandering off. She was out there somewhere, alone and frightened. The shepherd didn't think, 'Oh well, serves her right. The other ninety-nine are safe anyway.' No! He quickly piled up stones at the entrance to keep the others safe, and then set off once more, going back over the way he had just come.

As he went, he called to the sheep, listening carefully to hear if she was answering. But there was no sound except for a wolf howling somewhere, and one answering in the hills. He hurried on. It was a long way, back to where they had all spent the day. At last, he reached the hills and the stream. He called again and listened – and this time he heard an answer, a very faint bleating. He called again, and followed the sound of the reply. He was climbing now, struggling up the hill through the rocks. And there, at last, he saw the sheep. Her eyes were wide with fear. She knew there were wild animals close by. She tried to get to him, but she couldn't. Her fleece was caught in a thorny bush, and the more she struggled, the deeper the thorns tangled in the wool. The shepherd spoke quietly to her. She knew his voice. She knew she was safe now, and she lay there without moving while he untangled her. At last she was free. He picked her up, resting her weight over his shoulders, and set off on the long walk home. He was very happy and he sang as he went. Back at camp, he checked that she was all right, and that the thorns had not scratched her. Then he put her in with the others. 'Tomorrow,' he thought, 'I shall have a party to celebrate finding my sheep.' And he settled down to cook his supper, thinking about the food he could give his friends the next day.

Christians believe that this story is like a picture of God and his people. They believe God is like the shepherd. He wants everyone to be his friend. It doesn't matter that he already has a lot of friends. He is still really pleased when someone becomes his friend.

PRAYER

Thank you, Father, that you care about each of us, and that we are all important to you.

REFLECTION

Ask the pupils to think about how it feels when we find someone who wants to be our friend – someone who cares about us. Ask them to think whether they are a friend like this to other people.

28 Forgiving Others

You will need

- a chair and paper crown for the king
- a duster
- a book

Introduction

Discuss with the pupils what it means when we say we forgive someone. Ask them if they expect to be forgiven if they say sorry. Ask them if they would forgive other people if they said sorry to them. Would it depend upon what they had done in the first place?

Jesus told a story about people forgiving others. (As you tell the story, guide pupils playing the three parts so that they are acting out the story.) There are three main people in it – a king, and two servants. Choose these three: sit the king on his throne with the book open on his knee, and have one servant dusting over at one side of the acting space. The other one is to wait 'off stage'.

One day, the king was checking how much money he had. He found out that a certain servant owed him a lot of money – over a million pounds! He sent for the servant (bring on the servant with the duster) and asked him to pay him immediately. 'If you do not pay, I will have to sell your family to get the money!'

The servant knelt down in front of the king, and begged him to give him more time. 'I will pay you back every penny,' he promised, 'but I need more time!' The king felt sorry for him, and said he need not pay any of the money he owed him. The servant was very pleased. He got up, and left. But as he went, he met another servant. (Direct the first servant over to the second.) 'You owe me five pounds!' he said. The servant knelt down in front of him and begged him to give him more time, but the first servant refused. 'Throw this man into prison!' he ordered.

When the king heard what had happened, he was furious. 'I forgave you,' he said. 'You should have forgiven that other servant!' And he ordered his men to throw him into prison.

Ask the pupils why the king changed his mind about forgiving the first servant. Was it the servant's own fault? What should he have done? Discuss with them Jesus' message here – that if we expect others to forgive us, we should also forgive other people. Christians believe that God is always ready to forgive people for whatever they do wrong. They believe that God wants us to forgive other people too.

Note

This should not be seen by the pupils as a reason to allow bullying to continue. If anyone is hurting us, that is wrong and should be stopped straight away.

REFLECTION

Ask the pupils to think briefly about anyone they are angry with, and then listen as you say:

It is easy to expect others to forgive us when we say sorry. Sometimes it is harder to forgive them when they say sorry to us.

LINK

'Brothers and Sisters 2/3', *Families and Friends* section, pages 70 and 72

29 The Lost Son

Introduction

Ask the pupils if they have ever done something wrong and then realized that they have to say sorry for it. (Stress that you do not want to know what it was!) Sometimes when this happens, we are not sure what people will say to us when we say sorry. We wonder if they will forgive us or if they will be angry with us. Jesus once told a story about a teenage boy who felt like this. Jesus did not give him a name, but we will call him Reuben.

Core material

Reuben was bored! He lived on the family farm with his father and elder brother. 'I do nothing but farm work!' he moaned. 'I never meet anyone interesting! I've had enough of this life!' He asked his father to give him his share of the family's money. His father was upset. He loved Reuben and wanted him at home with him, but he could see that his son was not happy there. He gave him the money. 'At last!' Reuben said. 'Now I can begin to enjoy myself!' And he left home.

He travelled to a town far away from the farm, and found an expensive house to stay in. He began to hold long noisy parties every night, with the very best of food and drink. The people of the town realized that Reuben's house was a good place to be – plenty of free food and drink! But the money soon ran out. Reuben's new friends did not want to help him once he had no money. They left him by himself. He had to sell everything he had to buy food. But soon there was nothing left. The only job he could find was looking after someone else's pigs.

One day, he was so hungry that he almost ate the pigs' food! 'I shall have to go home and say sorry for leaving Dad and wasting the money,' he thought. 'Even Dad's servants were well looked after. Perhaps Dad will give me a job.' So he set off. He was worried that his father might be so angry with him that he would not even see him. He trudged on, weak and tired. At last, he turned onto the track that led to the farm. In the distance, he could see the farmhouse. But he could see something else as well. Someone was running down the track towards him. Was his father so angry with him that he was sending someone to stop him coming to the farm at all? He peered up the track – and realized that it was his father running to meet him.

As soon as he reached him, his father threw his arms round his son. Reuben tried to say sorry for what he had done, but Dad wouldn't listen. 'At last you've come home!' his father said. 'Every day I've watched and waited for you – and at last here you are.' Then he took Reuben home, dressed him in fine new clothes, and gave him a ring to wear as a sign that he was back home as his son. Then he organized a great party for him. 'My son is home at last!' he told people. 'Come and celebrate with us!'

Christians believe that the father in this story is like a picture of God. God's friends sometimes do wrong things, and make him unhappy, but Christians believe that God is waiting for them to say sorry, and that he will forgive them whatever they have done wrong. He can hardly wait to be friends with them again.

PRAYER

Thank you, Father God, that you are like the father in this story. You want people to be friends with you, and you are waiting for them to talk to you.

LINK

'Brothers and Sisters 2/3', *Families and Friends* section, pages 70 and 72

30 God the Superhero

You will need

- labels with the names of the superheroes below (see first paragraph below)
- labels with the 'titles' of God opposite

Introduction

Give out the labels for the superheroes below in order, asking the pupils to step forward and display their names as you read them out. Depending on the pupils, they could say their own speeches, or you can read them for them. If possible, you could ask your own class to decorate the names accordingly – or design a simple hat for each hero to wear.

Here are some superheroes:

SuperMemory: I can remember everything – even what you all had for breakfast!

SuperSummer: No one can think of a sum I cannot do – in one second!

SuperTidier: My bedroom is always perfectly tidy!

SuperPetowner: I never forget to feed my pets – or to clean them out.

SuperTemper: I never lose my temper – whatever happens.

Are these people real? Could anyone really be like this? None of us is perfect. We all do things wrong at some time. Of course, we can still do our best to do things properly, but sometimes we fail. This might be because we are only just learning to do something. It might be because we are tired. It might be because we don't have time. It might be because we forget what we are supposed to do. Adults are not perfect either. They forget things, lose their temper, run out of time, or find they do not know how to do something. At some time or other, all of us find something that we just cannot do, no matter how hard we try. But Christians believe that there is someone who can do anything, and who is perfect at everything he does.

LINK

'Questions: God the Superhero', *Music Assemblies* section, page 100

Christians believe that God is perfect. They believe that he never does anything wrong. They believe that he is like a superhero. Give out the names and ask the pupils to hold them up so the others can see them. Read out each sentence, stressing that these are Christian beliefs about God.

SuperFriend: God has promised his friends that he will never leave them.

SuperPetowner: God made all the animals. They and the earth belong to him.

SuperCarer: God has promised that he will always look after his friends.

SuperPower: God is so powerful that he made everything out of nothing.

SuperHelper: God has promised to help his friends when they need him.

SuperParent: God is like the best kind of parent. He always has time.

PRAYER

Read through the 'titles' of God again, and ask the pupils to choose one of them to think about for a few seconds. If appropriate, the pupils can be invited to say their own prayer silently, thanking God for being that 'Superhero'.

Note

Many children do not have a positive experience or image of 'fatherhood'. To allow them to imagine that God is like their own father may not be comforting or helpful. There is a need to present God as the best type of father the children can imagine, not necessarily the type they have experienced.

Christians believe that God is not just female or male. He embodies the best characteristics found in each gender. For ease of reference, they often refer to him as being male. Some pupils might like to discuss this issue.

31 Brothers and Sisters 1

Introduction

How many of the pupils have brothers and/or sisters? Ask for a show of hands, then say that you have a special job for the pupils who do not have brothers and sisters: they are to help you decide if the others are telling the truth or not when they answer some questions. Ask them to watch the others as they answer. Ask the others:

How many of you never argue with your brothers and sisters?
How many of you are never jealous of them?
How many of you never wish you had things they have?
How many of you are never mean to them?

Ask your helpers if they think the others were telling the truth.

When we live with other people day after day, they often get on our nerves – or even drive us mad! A family of brothers in the Bible would certainly agree with this. They were so annoyed with their brother one day that they decided to sell him! Here is the first part of their story.

Joseph had eleven brothers, and all of them except one were older than him. In those days, the older brothers were more important than the younger ones, so Joseph should not have been an important person at all – but he thought that he was the most important brother! 'Listen!' he said one day. 'I have just had an amazing dream. The sun and the moon and eleven stars all bowed down to me because I am so important. Isn't that wonderful!' His brothers were annoyed. They knew that the dream meant that they and their father would all bow down to Joseph – and they did not want to do that. They knew, too, that Joseph was their father's favourite son: their father bought him special presents like expensive clothes, and he did not make Joseph work as hard as they did on the farm. They were very jealous – but Joseph did not care how they felt.

One day, the brothers were working out in the fields. Their father sent Joseph out to see what they were doing. The brothers were pleased. 'This is our chance to get rid of this trouble-maker!' they said. Some of them wanted to kill him, but the eldest brother knew this would be wrong. He told them to put Joseph in a deep pit, and leave him there. Really, he hoped that he could rescue Joseph later. But before he could rescue him, the other brothers sold Joseph to some traders who were on their way to Egypt. They knew that these traders would sell Joseph as a slave when they arrived in Egypt. That meant that Joseph would belong to someone else, and would have to do everything he was told to do. The brothers went home very happy. They had got rid of Joseph and earned some money! 'We will tell our father that a wild animal killed Joseph,' they said. 'We will never see our brother again!'

But they were wrong!

Joseph's boasting and his brothers' jealousy caused great unhappiness for Joseph and his father. What about his brothers? Do the pupils think that they would ever feel sorry for what they had done? Was it a good or right thing to do?

PRAYER

Father, it is very easy to say or do things when we are angry that we are sorry for afterwards. Sometimes these things hurt other people. Sometimes we too are hurt and made miserable by them. When we are upset or angry, help us to think carefully before we do or say anything, so that we don't hurt ourselves or others.

REFLECTION

It is not easy to live with other people at times. We should remember, though, that we can annoy others just as easily as they can annoy us!

32 Brothers and Sisters 2

You will need

- a large sheet of paper with 'Families' written down the left-hand side
- a large sheet of paper with 'Friends' written in the same way
- felt-tips

Note

This assembly develops ideas introduced in the previous assembly – 'Brothers and Sisters 1'.

Introduction

Refer to the assembly (page 68) in which Joseph was sold into slavery by his brothers. We agreed that it is easy for families to annoy each other. But what happens next? Here are the first lines of a family argument.

'You're sitting on my teddy-bear, Daniel!' Tracey shouted.
'It shouldn't be here, should it?'
'You've squashed his nose!'
'Tough! It's so old it won't make any difference anyway!'
'Mum! Daniel's being horrible again!'

Talk about understanding other people's feelings and the importance of saying sorry. What if Daniel had said, 'I'm really sorry, Tracey. I didn't see him there. I'll help you straighten his nose.'? Discuss with the pupils whether they think this would have been enough to stop the argument. What would have happened if Tracey had answered, ' Yes you did see him! You did it on purpose. I hate you!'? Discuss the idea of forgiving someone who says they are sorry. Both things are needed – saying sorry and forgiving.

Show the pupils the sheet with 'Families' written on it. Explain that you want to make a list of some of the things that can make people happy in a family. We have said that 'saying sorry' to others is important. Write this next to the 's' of 'Families', pointing out that it begins with this letter. Ask them where the word 'forgiving' will go, encouraging them to match up its initial sound. When both are in place, recap on the importance of both saying sorry and forgiving.

Then show them the other sheet. We can upset our friends as well as our families by the way we behave, and we need to say sorry and to forgive them in just the same way. Ask the pupils where the words 'saying sorry' and 'forgiving' will go on this sheet. Point out that without the letters 'f' and 's', families and friends are not the same at all!

In the last assembly, we heard how Joseph was sold as a slave by his brothers because of their arguments. In the next assembly, we will find out what happened when they met each other again. Would the brothers be sorry for what they had done? If they were sorry, would Joseph forgive them? Would Joseph and his brothers be friends again?

PRAYER

Help us, Father, to be ready to say sorry to others when we have done wrong. Help us to be ready to forgive others when they say sorry to us.

REFLECTION

Is there anyone we need to say sorry to today? Perhaps there is someone who has said sorry to us who is miserable because we have not forgiven them. Can we do something about this today?

LINK

'The Lost Son' and 'Forgiving Others', *Parables* section, pages 64 and 62

33 Brothers and Sisters 3

Introduction

Note

This assembly develops ideas introduced in the two previous assemblies – 'Brothers and Sisters 1/2'.

Recap on the story of Joseph so far, and remind pupils of the importance of saying sorry, and of forgiving other people. We are going to hear the rest of Joseph's story. What do they think will happen when the brothers meet Joseph again? Some pupils can come and improvise what they think will happen and what will be said by Joseph and his brothers.

Life had been very hard for Joseph in Egypt. He was a slave, owned like an animal by someone else. He had to do everything he was told. He even spent a long time in prison, because someone told lies about him. But then God helped him to save Egypt from a terrible famine when there was not enough food for everyone. Without Joseph, many people would have died. So, at last, Joseph became an important person in Egypt.

Back at home, his brothers were short of food too. They had to go to Egypt to buy corn, and the person they went to see was Joseph! They didn't recognize him, but he knew them straight away. He had to find out if they were still as cruel and selfish as they had been. So he set a trap for them. He said that the youngest brother, Benjamin, had stolen a silver cup.

The brothers were terrified. They thought that this important man might kill Benjamin. They knew that, if Benjamin died, their father would be very miserable. 'Punish me instead!' one of them told Joseph. 'Do not hurt Benjamin in any way!'

When Joseph heard this, and saw how unhappy they were, he knew that his brothers had changed. They were worried about Benjamin and their father. They knew that they had been wrong when they sold Joseph, and they were sorry for what they had done. They did not want to hurt anybody else. They knew that their father loved Benjamin, but they were not jealous any longer. So Joseph told his brothers who he was. They were even more terrified! 'He will kill us all,' they said, 'because of what we did to him!'

But Joseph said, 'Don't be frightened. I know that what you did to me was wrong. But God has used me here in Egypt to keep many people alive. I can give you food too, and a home here where you will be safe. I forgive you for what you did to me.' So Joseph's brothers and father came to live in Egypt, and the family was together once more.

Christians believe that God helped Joseph and his brothers to be friends again. They believe that, even though things had gone very wrong for the family, God was able to bring good things out of their trouble and to help this family and many other people. Christians also believe that God can still help them like this today.

PRAYER

Thank you, God, for helping Joseph's brothers to see how wrong they had been and to be sorry for what they had done. Thank you, God, for helping Joseph to forgive his brothers. Thank you that you can still help us today when we fall out with each other.

LINK

'The Lost Son' and 'Forgiving Others', *Parables* section, pages 62 and 64

34 What Sort of Tree?

You will need

- enlarged copies of the family trees (see page 117)
- (optional) the leaves and fruits of the trees in the guessing game, but the clues can be used by themselves

Note

Care should be taken here to avoid suggesting that only a traditional 'nuclear' family can be represented by a family tree.

The completed and blank family trees will be needed in the next assembly – 'A King in the Tree'.

Introduction

Ask the pupils what happens to the leaves of many of our trees in autumn. Talk about the beauty of the changing colours, and discuss what stage the leaves on the trees are in at the moment: are they just beginning to fall, or are most of them already on the ground? Some trees do not lose their leaves in autumn. Ask if the pupils can think of any examples of these. If you wish, you can introduce the correct names for these two types of tree – deciduous and evergreen – and discuss what they mean, and why some trees get rid of their leaves at this time of year. Talk about the shapes of different trees, showing the shapes of the two trees on the sheets.

Core material

Tell the pupils you are going to see how well they know trees. Give them the following sets of clues, pausing after each clue to see if anyone already knows the answer. (If appropriate, discuss the fact that 'fruits' does not mean just the fruits we eat. It means the cases the trees produce to carry their seeds, so that other trees can grow.) Stress that some of the fruits from trees (and other plants) are definitely not for eating: they would make us very ill! (If you have the leaves and fruits, introduce them at a suitable point in each set of clues.)

1   This tree has leaves like big, spread-out fingers.
    It has the name of an animal in its name.
    In the autumn, children – and some adults – make a hole in the seed of this tree, thread string through it, and play a game with it.
    (horse chestnut, seed – conkers)

2   This tree can grow very tall.
    It is an evergreen.
    Its leaves are like needles.
    In the winter, many people have this tree in their homes.
    (Christmas tree – Norwegian Spruce, for example)

3   This tree can live to be very old.
    Its fruit sits in little cups.
    Ships were once made of its wood.
    An old story says that a famous outlaw (Robin Hood) once kept his food in one, and hid in another one.
    (oak, fruit – acorns)

4   This tree only grows where it is very hot.
    Its fruit grows upside down in very big bundles.
    Its fruit can be green, but is usually yellow.
    Its fruit is long, and we have to peel it before we eat it.
    (banana)

There is one tree we have not mentioned yet. Here are its clues.

5   It does not have any leaves.
    It does not have any fruit.
    It does not grow in the soil.
    It does get bigger and bigger, though.
    You are on it!

This tree is a family tree. Explain what one of these is, filling in some of the boxes on the first tree (i.e. without numbers) to create a fictional family (e.g. Tom; Mum; Dad; Grandma; Great-Great-Grandad). Use the = symbol, explaining that it means that two people married each other. Also, explain the line which shows someone is the child of the person(s) above them in the tree.

Explain that many people now spend a long time and travel all over Britain and even the world to try to fill in all the names of their family trees. They try to find out all they can about the people whose names they put onto the tree. Sometimes they find out surprising things about them. They might learn that someone famous was one of their ancestors (explain this word, referring to the tree). They can then boast about this ancestor, saying, 'Guess who I'm related to!'

REFLECTION

Ask them to think about their own families while you read:

So many people in our family – going back through many years. Some were like me: some were very different! What would we learn if we could meet them all? What would they think of us? We are all in the same family – even though some of them lived hundreds of years ago. Will people in the future find out all about us, so they can put our names on their family trees?

35 A King in the Tree

You will need

- the family-tree sheet you filled in and the blank sheet from the previous assembly – 'What Sort of Tree?'

Note

This assembly is the first of four assemblies about Joseph and his ancestors.

Introduction

Remind the pupils about family trees, showing them the one you made. People nowadays fill in their family trees just because it interests them. But to some people, their family trees are very important, and were even more important in the past. Royal family trees are very important. Talk about the line of succession of a royal family, and how important it is that everyone knows each person is a real member of the family. Some royal families can fill in their family tree for hundreds of years.

There is a very long family tree in the Bible. But it isn't the family tree of a king. It is the family tree of a very ordinary man called Joseph. Show the relevant sheet, explaining that there should be many more names on it than there are boxes. We are finding out about just a few of his ancestors. Put Joseph's name in Box 1, and explain the word 'ancestors', showing where their names will go. Joseph's family tree had some surprising people hidden in it.

Core material

One of the people in this family tree was a king, even though Joseph wasn't. The king was David, the king of the Israelites. He was a very great king. He won many important battles. He tried to be fair to his people, and to listen to God so that he knew what God wanted him to do. But David fought his first battle before he was a king, while he was still a young boy.

David's country, Israel, was at war. They were fighting the Philistines, and they were not winning. David's brothers were in the army, and one day their father asked David to take them some food. When he arrived at the battlefield, he was surprised to find all Israel's soldiers in the camp. Why weren't they out fighting? Then he heard shouting. He walked over to the edge of the hill, and looked over the valley to the hill on the other side. A huge man stood there. He was like a giant. He wore heavy, shining armour, and he was making fun of the Israelite soldiers. 'You cowards!' he shouted. 'Not one of you dares come over here to fight me! That God of yours can't be much good. Are you frightened he won't be able to help you?'

David was angry. How dare this man make fun of God! He went to Saul, the king of Israel, and told him that he would fight Goliath. Saul laughed. 'You?' he said. 'You're only a boy!'

But David said, 'I might only be a boy, but God is with me. He has helped me to kill wild animals with my sling to keep my father's sheep safe. He will help me today.' Saul gave him his own armour to wear – but it was so big and heavy that David couldn't walk in it! He took it off, and went down to the stream in the valley. There, he chose some round, smooth stones. He had his shepherd's stick and his leather sling with him.

Goliath was angry when he saw David. 'Do you think I am a dog, to be frightened when a boy comes to me with a stick!' he yelled. 'Today I shall kill you!'

'No, Goliath!' David shouted back. 'Today I shall kill you! You come to fight me dressed in armour, with your sword and spear. But God is with me and he will help me to fight you.' Then David put one of his stones into the sling. He ran towards Goliath, twirling the sling above his head. Then he let go of one end of it. The stone flew through the air, and hit Goliath in the forehead. And he fell to the ground, dead.

The Israelites realized that God was helping them. They attacked the other Philistines, and the Philistines panicked. 'If their God can help that young boy to kill our best soldier, he must be very powerful,' they said, and they ran away with the Israelites chasing them.

So one of Joseph's ancestors (or 'someone in Joseph's family in the past') was a king called David who had killed Goliath when he was still a boy. Put David's name in Box 2.

REFLECTION

The soldiers thought they were brave – but David was braver. Think for a few moments about being brave.

PRAYER

Dear God, David was only a boy. He knew that you could help him. But he had to trust you to help him. Thank you that you helped him, and that you can still help us when we face frightening times.

36 A Promise in the Tree!

You will need

- Joseph's family tree from the previous assembly – 'A King in the Tree'
- an apple pie and a spoon
- a large stone

Note

This assembly is the second of four assemblies about Joseph and his ancestors.

Introduction

Show the pupils Joseph's family tree again. So far, we have heard about David, a king. Not many of us will become kings or queens. But the next person whose name we will fill in became famous for doing something we can all do. She was called Ruth, and she lived before David. Ask which boxes her name could go in. She became famous for keeping her promises.

Core material

Talk about the meaning of 'promises', and ask for some examples of promises we might make to our families or to our friends. Ask the pupils if they know of any times when special promises are made – such as the promises made when boys and girls become members of the Scouting and Guiding organizations. Are there any adults who could demonstrate this, or Rainbows, Beavers, Brownies or Cubs who could tell the others their promise? Ask if any of them have heard the promises people make to each other when they get married. Give one or two examples from these. Discuss how easy or difficult it is to keep promises. Ask if it is important to keep the promises we make to other people, and why. Can they rely on their friends to keep their promises? Can their friends rely on them to keep their promises?

The promises Ruth made were not easy to keep. It would have been far easier for her not to keep them. But she did keep them. The promises were made to another woman called Naomi. Naomi was the mother of Ruth's husband.

Naomi did not live in her own country. She had moved to another country with her husband and her two sons when there was not enough food at home. She lived there happily for a while, and her sons got married to two women called Orpah and Ruth. But then her husband and her sons all died. Naomi decided it was time to go home to Israel. Orpah said goodbye to her, and went back to her parents' house. But Ruth refused to leave her. She said, 'Don't tell me to leave you or to let you go alone. From now on, where you go, I will go too. Where you stay, I will stay. Your people will become my people, and I will worship your God. I will not leave you until you die, and when I die, I will be buried next to you. And only death will ever separate us.'

So when Naomi set off on the long walk home, Ruth was there with her. Life was not easy for Ruth in Israel. The people there did not like the people of Ruth's country. They did not know Ruth, and they were not nice to her. The two women were very poor, and they were often hungry. When it was harvest time, Ruth set off early for the fields. There, she worked hard in the hot fields, collecting the grains that the workers had left behind, so she could make bread for Naomi and herself.

As she worked, the owner of the fields was watching her. This man was Boaz. He asked who she was. When he found out how she had left her own country to help Naomi, he told his workers to look after her. 'Give her food and water,' he said, 'and make sure you leave plenty of grain for her. Tell her to come to my fields every day during the harvest.' So Ruth was able to find food for Naomi.

Soon, she and Boaz came to love each other, and they were married: fill in her name in Box 3, and 'Boaz' in Box 4, reminding the pupils what the = symbol means in a family tree. They had a son called Obed (write his name in Box 5), and when he was grown up, Obed had a son called Jesse (Box 6). Help them to work out who Jesse's son was. So Ruth was David's great-grandmother.

REFLECTION

There is a saying about a promise, 'That's a piecrust promise.' This means that the promise was as easy to make as the pastry on an apple pie, and that it was as easy to break as it is to break the pastry in an apple pie with a spoon.

Show the children the apple pie and break the crust with the spoon, asking the pupils if their promises are like this. Then show them the stone, showing how hard it is.

No one could break this stone easily. Ruth's promises were as strong as this. Are theirs? Ask them to think quietly about their promises: can people trust them to keep them?

37 A Wise Man in the Tree!

You will need

- Joseph's family tree from the previous assembly – 'A Promise in the Tree!'
- felt-tips
- paper

Note

This assembly is the third of four assemblies about Joseph and his ancestors.

Ask the pupils some simple riddles, e.g.:

What do you say to start a teddy bear race? Ready, teddy, go!
What goes black, white, black, white, black, white? A penguin rolling down a hill.
What is yellow and goes up and down? A banana in a lift.

Introduction

If appropriate, you could ask them if they know any more. Riddles are a sort of question or puzzle. They are meant to make people laugh. It doesn't matter if we don't know the answer or get it wrong. But some questions and puzzles are not funny. Sometimes people are puzzled by things that are very serious. They might not know what to do, or they might be in some sort of trouble. They need to know the right answer and they need to get the answer right first time. What they need is someone who can give them advice about their problems and puzzles. Explain that the next man we are going to learn about in Joseph's family tree was famous for helping people with their problems. If anyone did not know what to do or needed advice, they would go to this man. His name was Solomon, and he was David's son. (Put his name onto the tree in Box 7.)

When David died, his son Solomon became king. Solomon knew that this was not an easy job. He had to look after all the people, and help them with all their problems. He had to defend his country from enemies and make sure everyone was safe. He had to make sure the country earned enough money for his people to have enough to eat. God asked him to choose a gift. 'You can have anything you want,' God told him. Solomon realized that this was like a riddle. He could choose the wrong answer. He thought about how difficult his new job was.

'I need help to do this job,' he thought. So he said to God, 'Please give me the gift of wisdom, so that I know how to do my job as king properly.' Solomon wasn't asking God just to make him clever. When the Bible says that someone has wisdom – or is a wise person – it means that they know how to live in the way God wants them to live. Solomon wanted to be wise so that he would know what God wanted him to do as king.

Soon, people in other countries heard about Solomon and about how wise he was. They heard that he ruled fairly and that his country was peaceful. They heard that people who had difficult puzzles to solve would get the right answer from Solomon. The queen of a country called Sheba heard about Solomon. She decided to visit him herself so that she could test him. It was as if she set Solomon a very difficult examination or test – and Solomon passed it because God was helping him. The Queen of Sheba returned to her own country telling everyone else that it was true – Solomon was a very wise man!

Solomon became famous, too, for his wise sayings. Choose one or two of these to tell the pupils and to discuss:

'Plans can fail if people do not listen to advice.' (Prov. 15:22)

'Working hard brings good things to people, but just talking about work doesn't do any good at all.' (Prov. 14:23)

'A friend stays a friend all the time.' (Prov. 17:17)

'Some people cannot be trusted. Trying to trust them to help you is like trying to chew with a wobbly tooth.' (Prov. 29:19)

'Hitting someone on the nose makes it bleed. In the same way, making someone angry on purpose leads to trouble.' (Prov. 30:33)

'If people want to learn more, they do not mind being told when they are wrong.' (Prov. 12:1)

REFLECTION

With the pupils, make a list of people they can go to for advice. Then ask them to think quietly about any puzzles and problems they have. Could one of these people help them with it? If not, could one of these people tell them who to ask?

38 Why was Joseph in the Tree?

You will need

- Joseph's family tree from the previous assembly – 'A Wise Man in the Tree!'
- felt-tips
- paper

Note

This assembly is the last of four assemblies about Joseph and his ancestors.

Introduction

Show the pupils the family tree, going over the names in order. Many years after Solomon died, Joseph was born (Box 1). Several people on the tree were famous for various reasons. But Joseph was just an ordinary man from a poor family. Why was Joseph's family tree written down in the Bible? What made him so important that people needed to know who his ancestors were?

Ask the pupils who they think is the most important person in the school; in the town/city; in the country. Who else is important? Write down some of their suggestions, one name to a piece of paper, and ask them to come and hold them up. Ask why they chose each of these people and what makes them important. They might be important because of who they are or because of what they do. Introduce the idea of a person's job making them important to other people – a school crossing warden, a teacher, a nurse. Add such people if necessary.

Joseph wasn't important to other people because of who he was. But he was important because of the job God gave him to do. At times, it was a dangerous job and it was hard work, too. God had chosen Mary to be Jesus' mother. Ask the pupils to tell you what they know about Mary. The Bible says that God was Jesus' father, but God chose Joseph to be Mary's husband, to look after her and Jesus, while he was a baby and a boy. While Jesus was still a baby, Joseph saved his life, and through all the years when Jesus was growing up, Joseph looked after him and kept him safe.

We hear a bit about Joseph in stories told at Christmas, but not much. Ask the pupils to tell you what they do know about him. This might include: he married Mary; he took her to Bethlehem; God told him that King Herod wanted to kill Jesus, so he took Mary and Jesus to Egypt; when it was safe, he brought them back to Nazareth; he was a carpenter and taught Jesus how to do this work too. Fill in anything they missed out. This is about all we are told in the Bible about Joseph. But if we think about these things, we will see that we know some other things about Joseph, too. We know he was brave. He kept Mary and Jesus safe when they were all in danger. He loved Jesus and looked after him, even though he was not his own son. He brought him up and treated him just as he treated his own sons. He taught him how to be a carpenter so that he could help him in his work. He loved Mary and married her even when other people might have been laughing at him and making fun of him because they knew Jesus was not his son. They thought some other man was Jesus' father. They thought Mary did not love Joseph. God knew that Mary would be a good mother for his son. He knew that Joseph would be a good father for him, too.

Christians believe that one of God's prophets, his messengers, said that God's special king would be born into the family of Jesse and David. They believe that Jesus was that king. Joseph was part of the family of Jesse and David, and was chosen to look after Jesus while he was too young to look after himself.

PRAYER

Father God, Joseph was no one special – just an ordinary man. But you chose him for a special job. Thank you that no one is just an ordinary person to you. We are all special, and you have a special job for us all to do.

LINK

Christmas section, especially 'Our Recipe for Christmas' and 'Another Christmas Recipe', pages 84 and 90

39 Our Recipe for Christmas

You will need

- slips of paper
- felt-tips
- 2 large bowls and several spoons
- tea towel
- weighed-out ingredients for your own recipe or the simple all-in-one fruit cake recipe given on page 116

Introduction

Talk about the school's preparations for Christmas, and the preparations being made at home. Perhaps one of the things being prepared at home or bought is a Christmas cake. Show the bowl and explain that you have the ingredients for a kind of Christmas cake – i.e. fruit cake – already weighed out. Some pupils can help you mix the ingredients together. If time allows, you could ask the pupils to tell you of any ingredients they know of, and add these as they are mentioned. If not, just talk about each ingredient as you add it. The mixture can be covered and put on one side ready to be cooked later in the day.

Many of the dishes we cook at home are like the Christmas cake – they have several ingredients. In the same way, Christmas has many ingredients for many people – for instance, decorations and giving presents. Show the pupils the other bowl, and explain that they are going to add the ingredients of Christmas to this bowl. It will be called a 'Christmas Mixture'. Write 'decorations' and 'presents' on two of the pieces of paper. Put these in the bowl, and invite two more pupils to help you mix them. Ask the pupils for more ingredients of Christmas. They can write or draw their own suggestions on the slips of paper. These can then be added to the mixture. As each is added, repeat its name to the other pupils.

When you think you have received most of the pupils' ideas, ask them to remind you whether anyone mentioned Jesus or the story of his birth. If not, introduce this now. Christmas is celebrated now (or give date) because it was thought Jesus was born at this time of year. Christians believe that he was God's own son, who came to earth as a baby. This is the story of the beginning of that first Christmas.

One day, when Mary was busy working in the house, an angel, one of God's messengers, came to see her. He had a very important message for her from God. 'You will have a baby soon,' he told her. 'He will be God's own son.' Mary was very surprised when she heard this, but she knew that God loved her and would look after her and his child. She was engaged to be married to Joseph, and God told him about this baby, too. Joseph married Mary, as God had told him to.

Their land was ruled by the Romans. The Roman Emperor ordered everyone to go to the town where their family first came from to put their names on lists so that the Romans could work out how many people lived in the country, and how much tax they could pay. Joseph belonged to the family of David (see pages 82–83) so he and Mary had to go to Bethlehem, where David's family had lived. Mary's baby would be born soon, but they still had to travel all the way to Bethlehem. It was a long journey, and they were both very tired when they finally arrived. Many other people were there, too, to sign their names. The only place Mary and Joseph could find to stay was in an animal shelter! But it was warm and dry, and much better than camping outside. During the night, Mary's son was born. Mary wrapped him warmly and Joseph filled an animal feed trough with soft clean hay. There, Jesus slept, warm and safe.

Ask the pupils what ingredients we have just heard about, starting them off with 'angel'. Write these on the paper, and add to the bowl. (This bowl will be added to in the following assemblies.) Perhaps the pupils can suggest someone to whom you could give the real cake.

PRAYER

Ask the pupils to watch as you stir your Christmas Mixture, and to think about the ingredients in it. Then ask them to listen to the prayer.

Thank you, God, for all the surprises of Christmas.
Thank you for the things we do every Christmas – such as decorating the room and eating good food.
Help us to remember why we do all these things, and to remember to thank you for the present you gave at the first Christmas.

REFLECTION

Ask the pupils to think about all the things others do at Christmas to help the pupils to enjoy it. Do they ever say thank you for these things, or do they take them for granted?

40 Good News!

Good News!

You will need

- the Christmas Mixture bowl from the previous assembly – 'Our Recipe for Christmas'
- slips of paper
- felt-tips
- (for reflection) recording of the 'Hallelujah Chorus' from Handel's *Messiah*

Introduction

Remind the pupils of the Christmas Mixture bowl. Explain that we are going to add more ingredients today. We heard about Jesus' birth. Today, we are going to hear about how the news of his birth spread. Sometimes, when we have news to tell people, we can hardly wait, but want to do it as soon as possible. Darren was like this. Here is a story about Darren and his good news. Ask some pupils to mime the action as you read. They will need to be in carer/child 'pairs', but standing separately to begin with. They will know what to do as they listen to you.

Core material

Every day, after school, the mothers and fathers, grandmas and child-minders stood outside the school doors. Every day, Darren's mother stood with them. Every day, she watched the other children coming out of school, coats flapping, books bursting out of folders, lunch-boxes spilling paper and orange peel on the ground. Every day, she watched as child after child set off home with mother or father, grandma or minder. And every day, she was left alone, waiting. Then, at last, Darren would appear. 'Hello!' he'd shout, happily.

'At last!' Mum would say. 'Everyone else came out ages ago. Where were you?' Then Darren would explain that he had been busy packing his bag or sharpening the pencils, or talking to Mr Foss about football, and he was very sorry, but he just hadn't realized how late it was. Mum would listen and smile. Darren would never be out early, she decided. He just couldn't hurry.

Then, one Monday, Mum was there as usual, waiting outside the doors with the others. (Pause while you direct the pairs to separate again.) They heard the bell – and next moment, there was Darren! Mum could not believe it. 'You're first!' she said. 'What happened? What's wrong?'

Darren laughed. 'Nothing's wrong, Mum,' he said. 'I've got some good news – and I couldn't wait any longer to tell you.'

'Well, I hope you have good news every day, then!' his mother said, and they walked home together as he told her all about it.

God had some good news to share at Christmas, and he couldn't wait to tell others about it either. Ask if any of the pupils can suggest what this good news was. *God* knew that his son had just been born in an animal shelter in the small town of Bethlehem, but no one else in Bethlehem knew about Jesus' birth except for Mary and Joseph. Who would God choose to tell his good news to?

There were the rich people in the town, and the rulers. There were the important people, and the ones who owned a lot of land. But God didn't choose any of these. He sent his messengers, the angels, to some shepherds who were looking after sheep in the hills. Shepherds were some of the least important people in the whole town. But God chose them to be the first to hear that Jesus had been born.

They were settled down for the night when suddenly a bright light shone out of the sky and dazzled them. They were frightened, especially when they saw an angel above them in the sky. But he said, 'Don't be frightened. I am here with very good news – for you and for all people. Tonight, down in Bethlehem, God's son has been born. He will save his people from the wrong they have done.' Then there were other angels there with him, all singing songs of praise to God because he loved people so much that he had sent his son. The song finished, and the shepherds were alone with their sheep on the cold, dark hillside. They hurried down into Bethlehem, and found Jesus. They worshipped God, kneeling down in front of this tiny baby. Then they returned to their sheep, thanking God for sharing his good news with them.

Hold up the bowl. What ingredients are there to add today? Ask the pupils to write or draw their suggestions, and add them to the mixture.

REFLECTION

PRAYER

The first Christmas came as a shock to the shepherds! They were not expecting to hear any angels that night! Ask the pupils to close their eyes and to imagine they are on the dark, silent hillside with the shepherds. Play an excerpt from Handel's 'Hallelujah Chorus'. Then return to the silence. At the end, if appropriate, read the prayer:

Everything was quiet. It was dark. But then, God, your angels came with the good news. Thank you that the news of Jesus' birth is still good news for many people.

41 The Wise Men's Story

You will need

- large sheets of paper with outlines of constellations on them (some examples are given on page 118)
- the Christmas Mixture bowl from the previous assembly – 'Good News!'
- slips of paper
- felt-tips

Introduction

Ask if any of the pupils like to look up at the sky and the stars on a clear night. Sometimes, people look at the stars and think that they make pictures and shapes. When there is a group of stars like this, it is called a constellation. Long ago, people made up stories to go with these pictures, and gave them names. Show the pictures of the groups of stars and talk briefly about their names and/or the stories told about them. Suggest that the pupils might like to ask a grown-up in their family to take them outside one dark, clear night, to see if they can see any of these. Stress that they must not go outside by themselves, though.

Some people spend a lot of time looking at the stars and studying them. If anything unusual or exciting happens – such as a new star appearing, or a star disappearing – these people notice straight away because they know the stars so well. When Jesus was born, there were people like this. They did not have the powerful telescopes we have nowadays for studying the stars, but they did know the stars very well. So when a new star appeared, they noticed it immediately. In the stories of their country, a new star as bright as this one meant that a great new king had been born. So they set off to find him. We often call them the Wise Men.

They travelled for many weeks, heading towards the new star which shone brightly ahead of them. At last they arrived in Jerusalem, the capital city of Judaea. Now Jerusalem was a great city, with a beautiful royal palace where the king of the country, King Herod, lived. The Wise Men thought that the new king would be here too, because the star now seemed to be right above them. So they went to the palace. When King Herod knew that they were looking for a new king, he was furious. 'I am the king here!' he shouted. 'No one else can rule here!' He pretended to help the Wise Men, and sent them to the small town of Bethlehem nearby. He said, 'Our people wrote long ago that a great king would be born in Bethlehem.' Then he asked them to come back and tell him where this king was, so that he could take presents to him too. But really he wanted to kill the new king.

The Wise Men travelled on, and soon realized that they had been wrong about the star. It was really shining over a small house in Bethlehem. And there they found the young child Jesus with Mary and Joseph. They knelt down before him because they knew that he was going to be a great king. They gave him the expensive gifts they had brought for him. There was gold because he was a king. There was sweet-smelling frankincense that priests used when they were worshipping God, because Jesus would show people how to be friends with God. And there was myrrh, which was used in burials. For Jesus would die when he was only a young man. That night, God told the Wise Men not to go back to Herod, so in the morning they returned home a different way. Joseph and Mary set off too – for Egypt, a land far away. God had told Joseph that Herod was trying to kill Jesus. So the family hurried away from Bethlehem, and lived safely in Egypt for several years, knowing that God was looking after them.

Add today's ingredients to the Christmas Mixture as before.

REFLECTION

PRAYER

Christians believe that Jesus with God created the stars. They believe that he came as a tiny baby.

Ask the pupils to think for a few seconds about these two things – the stars and a baby. Then read the prayer if appropriate.

He was so powerful that he made the stars.
He became so weak that he couldn't even feed himself.
Thank you, Jesus, for coming as a baby.

42 Another Christmas Recipe

You will need

- the Christmas Mixture bowl from the previous assembly – 'The Wise Men's Story'
- a large sheet of paper headed 'The First Christmas'
- Blu-tak
- felt-tips

Introduction

Show the pupils their Christmas Mixture and recap on the ingredients. In the last three assemblies, we have heard the story of the first Christmas, and we have added the ingredients of each part of the story. Now we are going to collect those ingredients onto one sheet to form a display.

Ask some pupils to come out one at a time to choose a slip of paper from the bowl until they are all taken. Explain that you are all going to collect the words or pictures that are part of the story of the *first* Christmas on the sheet of paper. The other ingredients, for *our* Christmas, go back into the bowl. (If time is short, remove these beforehand.) As the pieces of paper are stuck on the sheet, you can recap on the part played by each person, etc. Depending on the age of the pupils, they can order the ingredients chronologically, or you can take responsibility for this. The list will probably contain these people, places and things: angel, Mary, Joseph, Bethlehem, a stable or shelter, Jesus, the shepherds, angels, the star, the Wise Men, presents, Herod, Egypt.

Once the list is complete, explain to the pupils that there were other ingredients in that first Christmas, but that these were invisible ingredients. For instance, Mary's love for Jesus was important. Add these now in the appropriate places on the sheet, explaining who felt the emotions, for example, as you work. The pupils will need prompting for some of these. Suggestions might include: love, fear, dark night, warmth, sleep, jealousy, hatred, danger, care, protection.

REFLECTION

The Wise Men brought Jesus gifts that everyone could see. Some people brought him invisible gifts, such as love and protection. What invisible gifts could you give to your friends and families this Christmas? Would your parents like a gift of 'Help', for instance?

When the pupils have thought about this, you might like to take one or two suggestions and add them to the bowl as before.

Note

Choose which invisible ingredients – if any – to use with regard to the age and ability of the children.

43 Travelling to Jerusalem

You will need

- a small case or hold-all
- a selection of children's clothes – see below
- toiletries/towel, etc.
- book/game/toy

Note

This assembly should be followed by the next assembly – 'Lost in the Temple'.

Introduction

Ask the pupils to imagine that they are going on a visit to a big city about 100 miles away. Their visit will last two or three days. Discuss how they could get there. Ask them what they would need to take with them. Invite some pupils to come out and pack the case or bag for such a visit, commenting on what they include.

When Jesus was about twelve years old, he went on a visit like this one. Would the pupils' own families travel all together, or would the men travel separately from the women? In Jesus' country at that time, the men would all walk together, and the women would walk separately. Girls and the younger boys would walk with the women, and the older boys would walk with the men. Jesus would have had to take things like the ones we have packed. But he and his family had to take other things, too. Discuss how they would have travelled (by walking). They would have camped out on the way, so what else would they have needed to take? Talk about needing tents and bedding, and cooking equipment and food for the journey.

Jesus' family did not travel alone, but in a group of people from their own village. When they arrived, some of them would have stayed with relatives or with other people living in the city. But most of them would have camped out, for the city would have been full of other Jews who had travelled from every direction and even from other countries. For this was no ordinary visit. It was a special occasion. The people were travelling to Jerusalem to celebrate the Festival of the Passover in the Temple. Jesus and his family probably travelled to Jerusalem every year for the Feast of the Passover. This was when the Jews remembered how God had saved them from slavery in Egypt. But the visit we are told about in the Bible happened when Jesus was twelve. This meant that he was almost grown up, for Jewish boys were considered to be men when they were twelve or thirteen. This visit was different from all the others, and we'll find out how in the next assembly.

REFLECTION

Ask the pupils to look at the case or bag you packed and to think about a day out that they have really enjoyed. It could have been a day out to a place far away, or to somewhere nearby like the park or swimming pool. Ask them to think about how they looked forward to the outing, and how exciting it is to see new things or to do something they really enjoy. That is how Jesus felt as his family set off for Jerusalem.

LINK

'Travelling', *Music Assemblies* section, page 110

44 Lost in the Temple

You will need

- identifying objects/clothes for different people such as:
    - a toy stethoscope or syringe for a doctor or nurse
    - a pretend 'lollipop' for a crossing person
    - a piece of chalk or a boardwriter for a teacher
    - a computer mouse or disk for a computer expert
    - a spanner or other tool for a car-mechanic
- problems written on pieces of paper (see Introduction)

Note

This assembly follows on from the previous assembly – 'Travelling to Jerusalem'.

Introduction

Talk about asking people for advice if we have a problem or are confused. Who would we go to for advice? We would need somebody who knew about the problem we had. It would be no good going to a doctor and saying, 'Can you show me how to work my new cooker?' Explain that some pupils are going to pretend to be people who know a lot about one subject and can help others with their problems in that subject. Show each object, and help the pupils to guess what sort of expert would carry it. Select a pupil to play each part, lining them up at the front. Then choose other pupils to come out one by one with these problems, asking the others which expert each one needs:

'My car won't start.' • 'I need to cross this road to get to school.' • 'My tummy hurts.' 'I can't spell the word I need for my story.' • 'My computer's stopped working.'

Discuss what these experts would have said if their visitors had started telling them what to do, perhaps giving one or two examples. We usually go to experts when *we* need help, not when *they* do!

Recap on the last assembly, reminding the pupils that something happened in Jerusalem to make this visit different from the others. There were some men who worked in the Temple at Jerusalem who were experts. They believed that they knew all about God and about how he wanted people to live. Every day, other people went to these experts to ask their advice about many things and to be taught about God. When the people from Jesus' village went to Jerusalem each year, they would probably go to see these experts, to listen to their advice. But this year, things would be different!

Every year, Mary and Joseph joined the group of people travelling from Nazareth to Jerusalem. They enjoyed the chance to meet up with old friends and to take part in the special services at the Temple. When the festival was over, they packed up their belongings and set off for home. Jesus was not with Mary, but she did not worry, because she thought he was with Joseph and the other men. Joseph thought Jesus was with Mary. But when they stopped to make camp on the first night, they realized that Jesus was not with either of them. He was not there at all! They were very worried, and set off back to Jerusalem at once. They were tired, but for the next three days, they searched for Jesus all the time. At last, they found him. He was in the Temple! He was talking to the experts there. Mary and Joseph were frightened. Surely the experts would be annoyed at a young boy like this wasting their time. But they found out that the experts had been enjoying talking to Jesus. It had been interesting, and they had found out some new things about God! Jesus had been teaching the experts!

But Mary and Joseph told Jesus off. 'How could you frighten us like this!' they asked him. 'We didn't know where you were, and we were so worried!'

Jesus said, 'But I thought you would have guessed that I would be here. This is my father's house.' He meant that the Temple was where God was worshipped, and that God was his father. Mary and Joseph were surprised when he said this. They were reminded again of everything that had happened when Jesus was born and when the angel had told Mary about him. The family went home together to Nazareth, and there Jesus continued to grow up in the little village.

REFLECTION

Christians still talk to Jesus when they pray to him, and they believe they can still ask him to help them with their problems.

45 What was Jesus' House Like?

You will need

- a large sheet of paper
- an enlarged picture of Jesus' house (see page 119) or copy it onto another large sheet of paper
- felt-tips

Introduction

Introduce the assembly as one of a series that tells us about Jesus' life when he was a boy. Ask the pupils what sort of house they live in, and talk about the differences between these types (detached, bungalow, etc.). Draw simple outlines of these across the top of the paper. Unless they were very rich, people in Jesus' time all lived in the same sort of house. This was just a simple cube shape, with a flat roof and small windows with no glass. Draw this on the top of the other sheet (or show picture).

Ask the pupils what types of room a house has – such as a kitchen, a bedroom. Many of the houses in Jesus' village would have had only one room, which would have had a raised area at one end. The people would have shared this room with their animals. Probably a lot of the pupils share their home with animals – ask how many. Which animals do they have? Do any share their homes with goats and sheep and donkeys? Some of the families in Jesus' village did! Life must have been very crowded at times!

Jesus' house sounds as if it was very different from ours! Ask the pupils to name some of the things we have that they think Jesus would not have had in his house. But Jesus' house was just the same in many ways. It was his home, just as our houses are our homes, however big or small they are. A home needs certain things for people to be able to live in it each day: it needs cooking equipment, beds and bedclothes, lights, table and chairs, water. Invite some pupils to demonstrate these things in use. As each is demonstrated, help another pupil to demonstrate how it would be used in Jesus' home: his mother would sit on the ground, probably outside the house, to cook on a simple fire or stove; the family would sleep on the raised area, on thin mattresses which would be rolled up each morning with the blankets, and then propped up in a corner out of the way during the day; the lights would be small oil lamps which would stand on a high ledge or shelf; there would not be any table or chairs, but the family would sit on the floor; the water would not be in a tap, but would have to be fetched from the village well in large jars. Jesus would not think there was anything strange about his house – just as we think our houses are quite ordinary. To him, it was his home, where he learned and played with his brothers and sisters, helped his parents, and ate and slept.

REFLECTION

Christians believe that Jesus can understand how they feel as they grow up because he grew up as a child too, just like them.

Note

A wall display can be made, using information from this and the following assembly. Pupils can make plans of their own homes or rooms, and of a house in Jesus' village. Alternatively, younger pupils can draw the outside of their own home and of Jesus' home. Pupils could write pairs of sentences contrasting the two types of houses or life in them: e.g. Jesus slept on the floor. I sleep in a bed.

46 How Did Jesus Spend His Day?

You will need

- two large sheets of paper, both divided in half vertically, one sheet labelled 'boys' and 'girls'
- felt-tips

Introduction

Introduce the assembly as one of the series about how Jesus lived. Ask the pupils how they like to spend their free time: if they had tomorrow off school, what would they choose to do? What would any adults present choose to do? Perhaps some of these activities could be mimed for the others to guess. On the blank sheet, list or draw some of the activities mentioned down the left-hand column. This is how we like to spend our free or leisure time. But during term time, we do not have a choice about how we spend a lot of our time. We spend it at school! Ask the pupils about a typical school day, and write or draw each part of it down the right-hand column. So we now have an idea of how we spend our days, with the things we have to do, and the things we like to do. Of course, very often, we like doing the things we have to do, as well!

Core material

If Jesus and his friends had been asked to make two lists as we have just done, some of the things on the lists would have been very different, and some would have been the same. For a start, the boys would have made a very different list from the girls! Ask the pupils if there are any great differences between the days of girls and boys on our lists. Boys and girls now play the same games, and do the same work as each other. But it was very different when Jesus was a boy. Boys and girls both had very busy days – and they did not have many days off, either! But a boy's day was very different from a girl's day.

This is what a boy would do on a typical day (on the second sheet, enter words or simple pictures to represent each activity):

help on the family farm or garden – ploughing, planting, weeding and harvesting; younger boys would spend hours keeping birds away from the plants: others would look after the family's animals;

learning how their father did his work – their father might be a potter, a carpenter, a leather-worker, a metal-worker, a fisherman or a builder (choose one or two of these, and explain what they did); nowadays, children in this country can choose what they want to do when they grow up, but when Jesus was a child, boys usually learned their father's trade;

going to school – the boys had already done a lot of work but they still had to go to school: their school wasn't in a separate school building, it was at the synagogue – the building where the whole family went each Sabbath day to worship God. Here, the boys learned how to read the language their Bible was written in.

What about the girls? They had very different days! They would stay at home for much of the time, learning how to (enter some of these details on the chart): *do the housework, grind the grain, bake bread,* and *cook meals.* They would also have to *carry water from the well, wash the family's clothes* – and even *replaster the walls!* They did not go to school, but their parents would tell them about the history of their people and about God, just as they told the boys. Sometimes, girls helped in the fields too, and in looking after the animals.

Boys and girls did not have much time off. But they had every Sabbath day in which to rest, because the Jews were not allowed to work on that day. They would look forward to the great religious festivals like the Passover – just as some people look forward to Christmas. And they had their favourite games to play with their friends. Very young children would play make-believe games like weddings, just as young children do now. Children had homemade musical instruments to play on, and they had dice, balls, and rattles. So the list of the things they might have chosen to do is very like the list of the things we might choose to do nowadays.

Note

The teacher can select from the information in this assembly according to the age of the pupils and the time available. Pictures of children doing some of the jobs can be drawn and added to the display, or timetables can be written or drawn for pupils themselves and for the children of Jesus' time.

PRAYER

Father God, life was very different when Jesus was young. But at the same time, his life was just like life now in some ways. Children have always had to help their families, and to learn things which will help them when they are grown up. And children have always enjoyed playing. Thank you that there are so many different things to do and to learn.

47 Questions: God the Superhero

You will need

- the music of the song 'How?' (see page 102)
- the words for the pupils (see page 102)

Introduction

Ask the pupils some questions that are easy to answer, such as:

What colour is that wall?
What am I wearing?
What day is it today?

Then ask them some questions which are more difficult, but which they can still answer with some thought, such as:

What day will it be in two days' time?
One or two sums matched to their age group.

Then ask some questions which are impossible for them – or the adults present – to answer, such as:

How many stars are there?
What is [name] thinking about at the moment?
How many children are there in Australia with blue eyes?

Questions: God the Superhero

Some questions are easy to answer, some need a little bit of thought, and some are impossible for us to answer! Children often have a lot of questions to ask – and often they can't get proper answers for them! As we grow up, we learn the answers to many of our questions. But others are more difficult.

This song is about some of the questions asked by children. Some of the questions are asked by some adults, too! Read through the questions asked in the song, commenting on them as you go. Do the pupils know the answers to any of them? Are there some questions they cannot answer?

Read the chorus. Christians believe that God knows the answer to every question, including the impossible ones we thought about earlier, and that he made the things such as the sun, the clouds and the other things that puzzle some of us.

Teach the tune, preferably by an adult singing each line and asking the pupils to echo them. If necessary, concentrate on just one verse and the chorus.

PRAYER

Dear God, as we grow up, we find out more and more things that puzzle us. There is so much for us to discover and to learn about and to enjoy. Thank you that your world is full of mysteries and excitement.

LINK

'God the Superhero', *Parables* section, page 66

Song for **'Questions: God the Superhero'** *(page 100)*

How?

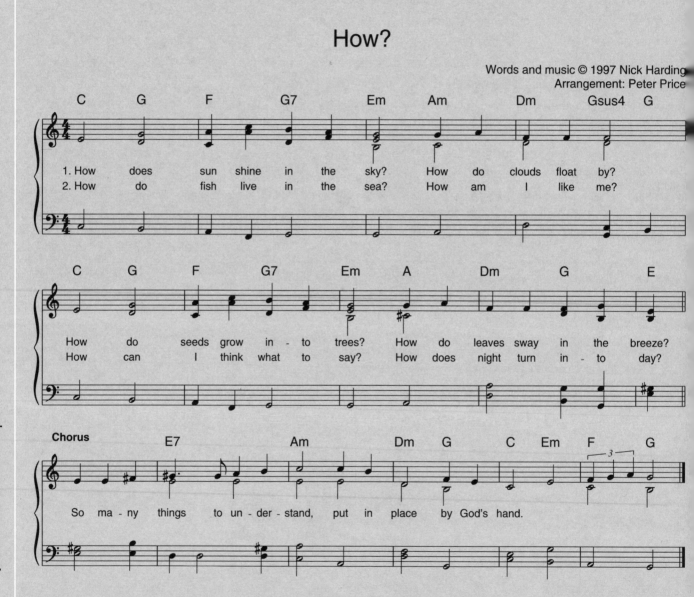

Words and music © 1997 Nick Harding
Arrangement: Peter Price

Song for **'Harvest: Teamwork'** *(page 104)*

Harambee

Words and music © 1992 Deirdre Madeley

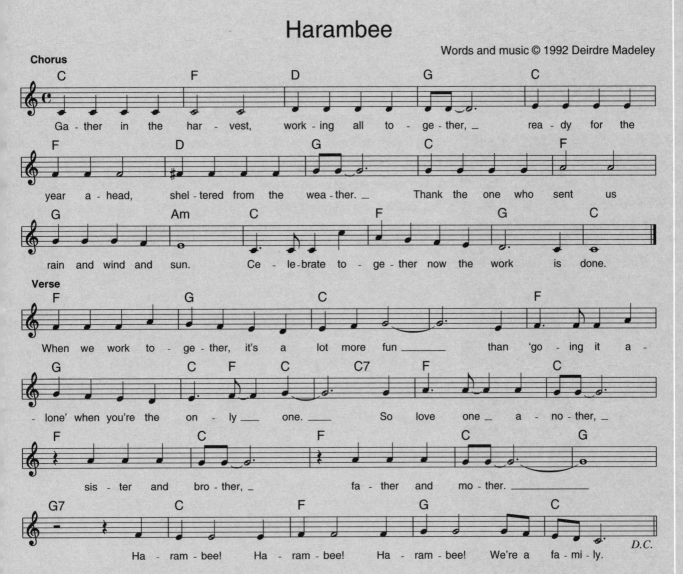

48 Harvest: Teamwork

You will need

- the music of the song 'Harambee' (see page 103)
- the words for the pupils (see page 103)

Introduction

Conduct a quick survey to find out the pupils' favourite sport. Is it a team sport or an individual sport? Talk about the difference between these two. In a team, the effort and hard work is shared, and so is the victory. If a very good football player was in a team where no one else cared about winning at all, would he be able to score many goals? Talk about teamwork – everyone working together. Members of a team do not try to win just so that they become famous. They work together so that the whole team can win.

Some schools have mottoes. Talk about your school's motto if you have one. If not, just explain what a motto is. Kenya is a country in Africa. It has a motto which means 'Working together'. Their word for this is 'Harambee'. Ask the pupils to say this with you. When we say 'Thank you' at harvest for the food we enjoy each day, we are really saying thank you to a team of people who bring us our food. (Refer to the assembly on page 8, if appropriate.) Ask them who helps to bring food to us: they might mention transport workers, fishermen, shopkeepers, farmers, etc. Christians believe that there is another, very important member of the team, and he is God. They believe that it is God who makes the seeds grow into plants, and sends the rain and the sun to help them grow. This is a song based on the idea of 'harambee': it talks about some of the people who bring us our food. Read the words of the song, and then teach the pupils the tune.

PRAYER

Thank you, Father, for the food we eat each day. Thank you for all the people who help to bring us that food. Thank you for your care and power which make the seeds grow each year.

LINK

'Sukkot', 'Harvest 1' and Harvest 2', *This Time of Year* section, pages 8, 10 and 12

49 The Good Shepherd

Note

This assembly can follow the assembly on page 58 about Jesus being the good shepherd. It can also be linked with the assemblies on pages 32 and 38 as these tell the stories of some people in India. It can be introduced with the idea that this Christian song comes from India and uses an old Indian tune. Christians in that country might sing it.

You will need

- the music of the song 'Jesus the Lord Said' (see page 108)
- the words for the pupils (see opposite)

Introduction

Remind the pupils of the assembly that talked about Jesus saying he was a shepherd or introduce this idea now. Recap as necessary on the meaning of this, thinking about the dangerous life the sheep would have had without the shepherd being there to help them.

Christians believe that Jesus is like a shepherd to them all the time. But there are some times when they really need him to act as a shepherd for them. Encourage the pupils to think about some of the times when Christians might be extra glad to remember that Jesus is their shepherd. Christians in India wrote a song to remind themselves of some of the things Jesus said. One of the verses reminds them that he said he was their shepherd. The words are very easy and repeated. Read the words to the pupils. Then teach this verse, preferably by the listen and echo technique.

Verse from 'Jesus the Lord Said'

Jesus the Lord said: 'I am the Shepherd,
the one Good Shepherd of the sheep am I.
   The one Good Shepherd of the sheep am I,
    the one Good Shepherd of the sheep am I.'
Jesus the Lord said: 'I am the Shepherd,
the one Good Shepherd of the sheep am I.'

REFLECTION

Ask the pupils to imagine they are sheep lost in a wild country at night. Ask them to imagine how they would feel if they heard their shepherd coming to find them.

This is how Christians feel when they are unhappy and they remember that Jesus is with them.

PRAYER

The pupils could sing the song quietly as a prayer.

LINK

'Jesus the Shepherd' and 'The Lost Sheep', *Parables* section, pages 58 and 60; 'Have You Got Any Water?' and 'Our Dream Village', *Other Children* section, pages 36 and 32

Song for **'The Good Shepherd'** *(page 106)*

Jesus the Lord Said

Words: anonymous, translated Dermott Monaha
Music: Urdu melody, arranged Geoff Weave

Song for **'Travelling'** *(page 110)*

God Goes with Us

Words and music © 1996 Nick Harding

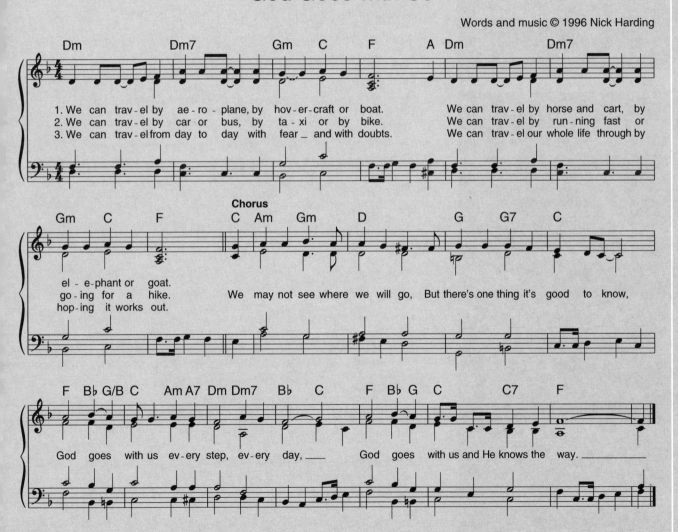

1. We can trav-el by ae-ro-plane, by hov-er-craft or boat. We can trav-el by horse and cart, by
2. We can trav-el by car or bus, by ta-xi or by bike. We can trav-el by run-ning fast or
3. We can trav-el from day to day with fear and with doubts. We can trav-el our whole life through by

Chorus

el-e-phant or goat.
go-ing for a hike.   We may not see where we will go, But there's one thing it's good to know,
hop-ing it works out.

God goes with us ev-ery step, ev-ery day, _____ God goes with us and He knows the way. _____

50 Travelling

You will need

- the music of the song 'God Goes with Us' (see page 109)
- the words for the pupils (see page 109)

Introduction

Ask the pupils to think silently about how we travel to different places. Ask some of them to come and mime the type of transport they have thought of. Make your own notes about the methods mimed. When you have several on your list, introduce the song. Read through the first two verses more than once if necessary. Ask if there are any methods mentioned here which the pupils hadn't thought of. If so, ask pupils to mime them with all the methods mentioned in the song are on your list.

We have listed ways of travelling. These are all ways of moving from one place to another. Some of us have made journeys in some of these ways, but is there anyone here who has journeyed in a goat-cart or on an elephant? The writer of this song was thinking about another type of journey – a journey that all of us are on all the time.

Read the last verse and the chorus. He was thinking about the way we are all travelling through our lives. We are all growing a little older each day. As we grow up, we will meet good times and happy times, sad times and lonely times. Sometimes life will seem easy and sometimes life will seem hard. Life is like a journey. Sometimes we feel we are getting somewhere and making progress, at other times we feel that nothing is happening.

The writer of the song knew that sometimes this journey through life can be hard and worrying. But he is a Christian, and he believes that people can ask God to go on this journey with them. He believes that God already knows where people's journeys are going. He believes that God will stay with his friends for the whole of the journey, and that he won't leave them when the journey is difficult.

Teach the pupils the song, preferably by them echoing someone singing it. If time is short, omit the second verse until a later date. Younger pupils can just join in for the chorus.

PRAYER

Ask the pupils to listen while you read the chorus to them.

LINK

'Travelling to Jerusalem', *Jesus' Boyhood* section, page 92

Music Suggestions

These are suggestions of songs for each section in the book. If they are not suitable for a school, others can be used.

BOOKS USED AND ABBREVIATIONS

JP1   *Junior Praise 1* comp. P. Horrobin & G. Leavers, Marshall Pickering, 1986

JP2   *Junior Praise 2* comp. P. Burt, P. Horrobin & G. Leavers, Marshall Pickering, 1992

ChPr   *Children's Praise* comp. G. Leavers & P. Burt, Marshall Pickering, 1991

All   *Alleluya!* chosen by D. Gadsby & J. Hoggarth, A. & C. Black, 1991

C&P   *The Complete Come and Praise* comp. G. Marshall-Taylor, BBC, 1994

BBP   *Big Blue Planet* ed. J. Jarvis, Stainer & Bell and Methodist Church Division of Education and Youth, 1995

Jump   *Jump Up if You're Wearing Red!* National Society/Church House Publishing, 1995

Cel   *A Year of Celebration* McCrimmon, 1995

THIS TIME OF YEAR

At harvest time **JP2**

I like the sunshine **BBP**

How beautiful **BBP**

I love the sun **ChPr**

Autumn days **C&P**

Pears and apples **C&P**

Round, round, round **C&P**

We thank you, Lord **C&P**

Sukkot **C&P**

Someone's brought a loaf of bread **JP1**

Thank you, Lord **Cel**

MEMORIES

The journey of life **JP2**

One more step **JP1.** See assembly on page 50

Get up out of bed **Jump**

Morning has broken **C&P**

Always remember, never forget **BBP**

I nearly forgot **BBP**

OTHER CHILDREN

Would you walk by **JP2**

Keep a light in your eyes **BBP**

He's got the whole world **C&P**

What colours God has made **JP2**

When the rain falls down **ChPr**

Have you heard the raindrops **C&P**

Waves are beating **C&P**

I love the sun **Cel**

SENSES: HEARING

Praise the Lord with the sound of a drum **ChPr**

I listen and I listen **C&P**

I'm very glad of God **JP1**

I've got eyes to see **Jump**

God is good to me **Jump**

I use my eyes **Cel**

PARABLES – GOD AND JESUS

One and two and three and four **JP2**

If you climb **Jump**

The Lord, the Lord **BBP**

It's hard to say I'm sorry **BBP**

God, you hold me like a mother **BBP**

I look out through the doorway **C&P**

When I go to the animal zoo **ChPr**

The Lord's Prayer **C&P**

When I needed a neighbour **C&P**

FAMILIES AND FRIENDS

A naggy mum **JP2**

God loves you **JP2**

Joseph was sold as a slave **JP2**

Think of a world without any flowers **JP1**

Our school is a happy place **Cel**

God is good to me **Jump**

Round and round the circle goes **Jump**

Playing, running **Jump**

TREES

See *Christmas* suggestions and

Only a boy called David **ChPr**

Wherever you go (first verse) **BBP**

CHRISTMAS

Christmas is a time to love **JP2**

Crackers and turkeys **JP2**

Come and join the celebration **JP2**

We have some news to bring **ChPr**

Here we come to Bethlehem **ChPr**

Mary had a baby **C&P**

An angel came from heaven **Cel**

JESUS' BOYHOOD

Jesus in the Temple **ChPr**

Jesus is the best friend **ChPr**

Paul's souvenirs for
'Memories 3' *(page 24)*

Make enlarged photocopies, or hand draw these pictures on large sheets of paper.

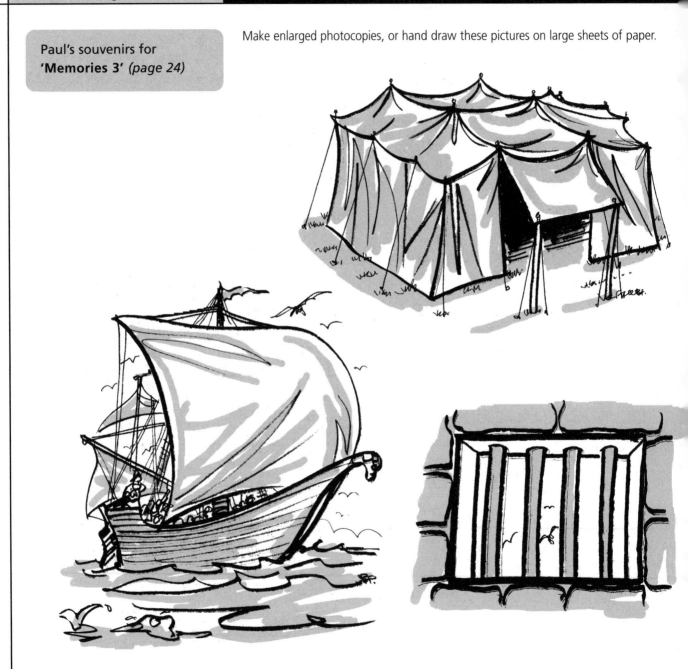

Paul's souvenirs for
'Memories 3' *(page 24)*

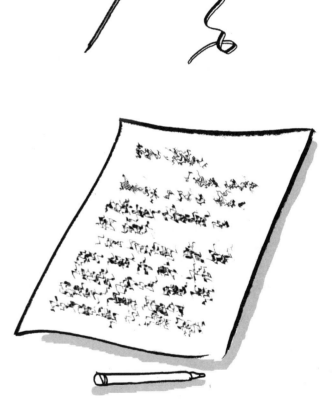

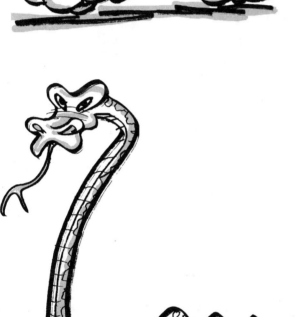

Operation Christmas Child logo for **'Operation Christmas Child'** *(page 40)*

Recipe for all-in-one fruit cake for **'Our Recipe for Christmas'** *(page 84)*

2 eggs

their weight in:

    self-raising flour

    sugar

    margarine

    mixed dried fruit

    glacé cherries, washed and dried

2 tbsp milk

Mix ingredients thoroughly and bake at 180 °C/gas mark 5 for 20–30 minutes.

Family tree for **'What Sort of Tree?'** *(page 74)*

Joseph's family tree for **'What Sort of Tree?'** *(page 74)* and the next four assemblies, on Joseph and his ancestors *(pages 76, 78, 80 and 82)*

The second tree contains boxes labelled:

3 = 4

5

6

2

7

1

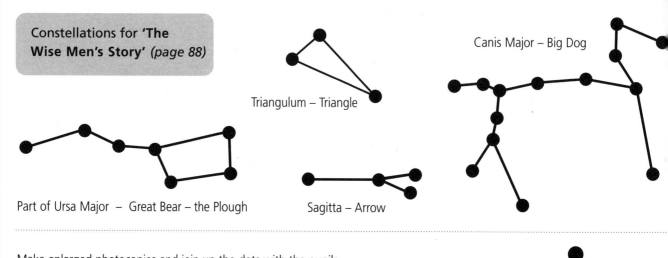

Constellations for 'The Wise Men's Story' *(page 88)*

Triangulum – Triangle

Canis Major – Big Dog

Part of Ursa Major – Great Bear – the Plough

Sagitta – Arrow

Make enlarged photocopies and join up the dots with the pupils.

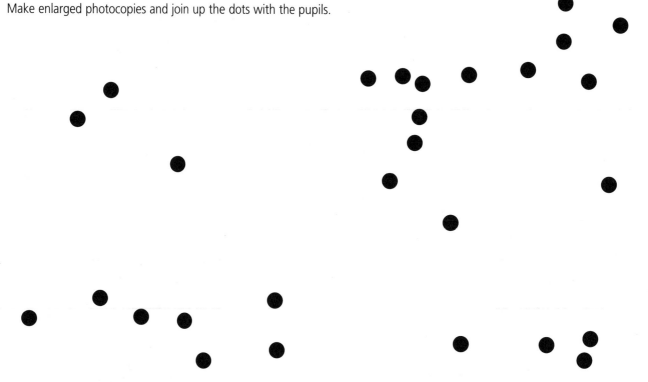

Biblical house for **'What was Jesus' House Like?'** *(page 96)*

People and Places Index

Thematic Index